BLITZED!

BLITZED!

THE AUTOBIOGRAPHY OF
STEVE STRANGE

ORION

DEDICATION
To a very special, kind and lovely person,
my grandmother, Gladys Price.
I love you Nan.

First published in Great Britain in 2002 by
Orion Books Ltd.
Orion House, 5 Upper St Martin's Lane,
London WC2H 9EA

Pictures supplied by
London Features Ltd., Rex Features Ltd., Gabor J. F. Scott.

A CIP catalogue record for this book
is available from the British Library

ISBN 0 75284 7201

Typeset by Selwood Systems, Midsomer Norton

Printed in Great Britain by
Butler & Tanner Ltd, Frome and London

FRONT COVER
Clothes by Vivienne Westwood, London
Hat by Stephen Jones, London
Hair by Derek Hutchins, Smile, London
Hair colour by Mac, London.

CONTENTS

ACKNOWLEDGEMENTS

To say it has been turbulent and hard writing this book is quite an understatement. It has been a rollercoaster emotional ride but I would really like to thank so many people for spurring me on and making me laugh so hard that tears would run down my face. Reminiscing with Rosemary Turner, Wendy May and Monica Gienita and, although reduced to tears on many occasions, my mother Gill and sister Tanya who are now happy that I am finally at peace with my life. (I'm so sorry for the hurt and pain I put you through – it won't happen again.) Chris and Tanya, I'm so pleased that you've given me two beautiful nephews, Kyle and Conor. I am also pleased that Jeanette and I have got our friendship back again. Talking of friendships, I love the new grown-up Boy George (the claws are not so long). Good luck with your new play Taboo and I'm really happy to have helped you. Whilst writing this book the projects that have blossomed are Chasing the Dragon (I get the digs in first) at Opium with Rose and Dylan and I'm really looking forward to collaborating with the Siren Suite's Matthew Glamorre. I shall also be rediscovering my friendship with the beautiful Miss Dee and cannot wait to kick off our new night and what, I hope, will be the new hot London club, Rouge (it will be the first time we've worked together). My life, like most people's, has had its share of ups and downs and I've probably brought the downs upon myself, but these things are sent to try us and I think I've grown up a hell of a lot in the last four years (not too grown up of course). I would like to thank Mark and Vincent and his beautiful wife, Wendy, for giving me my confidence back and for spurring me on with the writing of this book. I've tried to keep this book as 100 per cent truthful as possible but some things I have had to leave out, especially thinking about the family of people mentioned in my story.

Just before this book was going to print I broke a bone in my foot. This put me completely out of action and really made me realise how much we take for granted. It made me think how much hurt there is in the world and how I would really love to get involved in charity work to help the less fortunate. (If anyone is reading this, I'm available.)

So, before I finish, I would like to say that I've never been judgemental, as I believe we all have skeletons somewhere in the cupboard and that people who live in glass houses shouldn't throw stones.

Just one last important thank you, and that is to Bruce Dessau. Thank you for putting up with my erratic time-keeping and the cancelled meetings. With me sometimes you need the patience of a saint. I hope, like me, you think it has all been worthwhile. I thank you from the heart for all your hard work.

Thank you to whoever you are for buying this book.

The New Wave that Made the Punks Look Normal

Tuesday night. February 1979. 9pm. Covent Garden. Blitz.
'No, I'm sorry, you can't come in. You're not blonde enough ...'

For £1 you can have a ticket to the time of your life in the club of the moment. As long as you've got the right look. I'm vetting the queue, sorting the well groomed wheat from the clodhopping chaff. My hair is piled high and painted white. I'm wearing silver spectacles, a cowboy hat and a Victorian suit, with a silver-topped cane by my side.

Everything is running like clockwork. Rusty Egan is spinning David Bowie's Heroes back to back. George O'Dowd, the cloakroom boy who would soon reinvent himself as Boy George, is bitching and cursing everyone. Inside, the packed house is dancing, or at least trying to dance. There isn't a lot of room for self-expression; the dance-floor is about the size of a postage stamp. Swing an artful elbow and you are liable to hit a nearby reveller in the ribs. A safer bet is to stand by the bar, make a can of lager last all night and eye up the opposition. This club isn't about gyrating. It's about looking good and looking different. Watching each other to see who has come up with the more original outfit. Marilyn in his figure-hugging Monroe dress? George in his nun's outfit? David Claridge and Daniel James dressed as Thunderbirds puppets? But Blitz is much more than just a fancy dress party, it's the poseurs' paradise or, as the tabloids would have it, 'the new wave that makes the punks look normal'.

To look at us you'd think we were lords and ladies to the manor born, the cream of London's *demi-monde*. Diamante here, trowelledon eye-liner there. And that's just the men. Androgyny rules. And there is not a designer label in sight. Each unique outfit has been created by a mixture of initiative and cheek. Spend the day scouring the Oxfam shops round the back of Bond Street for expensive cast-offs, then nip to the make-up counter of Selfridges at 6pm for some free samples.

If the queue to get into Blitz stretches around the block towards Holborn station, the queue for the ladies' loo isn't much shorter. When you've spent all afternoon getting your hair to stand up vertically, your first port of call is the mirror to check that every strand is in place. 'You look lovely tonight, darling.' 'You do, too.' Then you spot a friend by the bar and you are off to peck them on the cheek and greet them with the same refrain.

Dressed to the nines, there might have only been 200 of us, but we were ready to take on the world. The following morning most of the people there would be back in their lecture hall or down at the dole office, signing on. The aspiring designers, journalists and entrepreneurs that in the eighties and nineties would make their mark in Thatcher's Britain and beyond saw the club as their natural rallying flag. Punk rock might have seemed like the biggest thing in my life when I was following The Sex Pistols around, but I had soon got bored with it. We took the punk situationist ethic of 'be reasonable, demand the impossible', but instead of forming rock bands we took over the whole of the capital's culture. In a year, even the future Princess of Wales would be partial to a few New Romantic frills.

Punk was not even a dress rehearsal for this. London had seen nothing quite like Blitz. When I think of London in the late seventies I think of a cold, grey place. Pubs closed in the afternoon. It was as if England had got through World War Two but, after a brief respite in the sixties, had never quite got round to dusting itself off. The most exotic meal you could get was a Chinese takeaway. Like Bucharest on a Wednesday night in September, everyone shuts up shop and goes back to their suburban semi, pulling together the lace curtains. The only lace curtains at Blitz were the ones people wore. Blitz made London swing again. And it was my baby, including the fame that came with it. Blitz was not just a club. It kick-started a whole new youth culture. In fact, it did even more than that. The youth of the world today don't go to pubs and bars at the weekend. They go to clubs. Until Blitz, clubs were discos – a fringe option. When I started to set up one-night events with Rusty I wasn't just starting a sub-culture; I was starting a leisure revolution.

CHAPTER ONE
STEVE HARRINGTON

My parents were always very stylish. The abiding image that I have of them comes from a picture they used to have on the wall at home, taken soon after their wedding. My father is in an immaculate Italian-style three-button jacket and drainpipe trousers. And my mum is next to him with back-combed hair, flicked up at the side with a bow on top, wearing an amazing black mini-dress with a see-through midriff. As I said, they were always stylish.

My father, John Harrington, was very regimental, right down to the creases in his trousers being spot-on. Nothing could be out of place. He paid attention to every detail. His suits had to be ironed to perfection, even if he had only worn them once. He would hold the collars up to the light to check that they were clean. They didn't have a lot of money but that didn't mean they couldn't look smart.

My mother, Gillian Price, was born and raised in south Wales. She met my father at a Catholic church dance. After the service they used to take the pews out and everyone would dance. They married when they were still teenagers. In the picture they look like the perfect couple.

I was born in south Wales on 28 May 1959. But when I was a baby my father joined the army. The Harrington family packed its bags and went on the march. We moved to his base in Aldershot. It was a rude awakening for mum. She remembers getting there at six o'clock in the morning after dad had been driving all night: 'I arrived in the square as all the lights were going on. All I could see were huts. It seemed like a prison camp.'

Dad was a paratrooper, a typical military man who believed in strict discipline. I was lucky that my mum was always there for me. Every time he tried to make me do something I didn't want to do, she would be there trying to stop him. But I was his son and he was determined to make a man of me from the start. He was a real storm-trooper. There was no room for sentimentality. The first thing I can remember is my red scooter. I loved that scooter. I was three years old, it was the first thing I ever owned, and I wouldn't let it out of my sight. I always wanted to bring it into the house after I'd finished playing outside, but my dad would make me leave it outside. I would cry my heart out. He didn't care.

Although he was not a sergeant major he behaved like one at home. I think he treated us in the same way that his sergeant major treated him. Everything had to be in its place. He made sure I was always smart: dressed neat and tidy, hair brushed with a little quiff sticking up. As mum and dad were married they were able to live just outside the base in Aldershot, but I don't think army life was a very happy time for mum. Dad was away a lot and mum didn't socialise much. She worked hard looking after me and got a secretarial job to top up their income. I can't remember much about Aldershot, except that I never really liked it. What sticks in my mind is the sound of aeroplanes flying low on the way in to land at Farnborough. They would scream overhead and I'd run into the house with my hands over my ears, burying my head in mum's apron.

The one thing I did like was music. I think I got that from my parents. With the extra cash coming in from mum's job they could start to treat themselves to life's little luxuries. The first thing my mum ever bought was a radiogram. Elvis Presley, then The Beatles. There was music wherever we went. My parents were only teenagers themselves when I was born and had to concentrate quickly on supporting a family. People had to grow up fast in those days, but they always loved pop music.

Things were more relaxed when dad was away. He was always over-protective, as if he didn't trust us when he wasn't around. In fact when he had to go overseas when I was about one year old he made us stay with his mother and father in Rhyl, north Wales. Mum used to work in their grocery shop with my father's younger sister Patricia, and I played with his other younger sister Lorraine. Although she was my aunt she was only about a year older than me, so we were more like brother and sister.

We didn't spend long in Aldershot. Dad decided to leave the army, although I don't think the army ever left him. When I was four he bought himself out and we all moved to Rhyl. Or to put it more accurately, mum bought dad out. The hard-earned cash she had been saving to put towards a house went on getting him back into civvies.

When we first arrived back in Wales, we lived with dad's parents and their children above their shop. My grandfather Patrick used to take me very early on Monday mornings to Liverpool market to get the groceries for the day. The most exciting part of the week was going through the Mersey Tunnel in his old Bedford van. For a few minutes we'd be in this strange hole in the ground. We could imagine emerging in a different place altogether.

Lorraine and I used to hang around together, but she had a different attitude to my dad when he had a go at her. She would answer him back: 'You're not my dad,' she would shout, but I couldn't, I was too scared of him. Lorraine was very good at dealing with my dad. She'd nick a few pounds from his wallet sometimes if she saw it on the table and dad was out of the room. I'd copy her but I was always terrified of being found out. Of course, dad always seemed to have money in his wallet for himself, for the pubs and the clubs. Like a lot of women in those days, mum was left to scrimp and save and be practical. Without mum's hard work and sacrifices they would not have been able to scrape enough money together to move out from their in-laws and buy a bungalow in Kimmel Bay, just down the coast from Rhyl. Mum always worked and there was plenty of work around in those days. As soon as we got to Rhyl she got a job in the council offices and we had to live on her money while he spent his.

Everything in the house in Wales was run as if he was still in uniform, barking orders at us and expecting every command to be followed to the letter. Disobedience deserved a smack. He had a thing about eating the right food. He would always try to make me eat butter beans, which I hated. When he wasn't looking I would put them in my pocket and try to flush them down the toilet. Except that they wouldn't flush and when he saw them he gave me another good hiding.

Dad was a big, strong man so he decided to work as a bouncer in the local clubs. They weren't discos back then, they were dances. On a Saturday night young men in search of fun and maybe, if they were a couple of years older, a wife would put on their finest clothes, brush their hair, rub Brylcreem in it and check themselves in the mirror. Then off they would go into town and flash a smile as they walked past my father. You'd either have to be very drunk indeed or completely mad to start an argument with him. He could always handle himself.

The trouble was that he was tough all the time. There was no let-up. He behaved like a bouncer at home too. When I went out to play I always had a curfew. If I wasn't back on time he would come looking for me. He'd drag me back by the scruff of my neck and once inside the house would spank me, putting me over his knee and giving me a good hiding while mum would be crying because she didn't agree with the way he treated me. My father's brutal attitude to life was that you had to confront your worst fears and either sink or swim. Sometimes he meant this literally. When I was five he took me down to the local swimming pool. I didn't have a lesson, he just picked me up and threw me in at the deep end. His theory was that this was the best way to learn to swim. I managed to splutter and keep my head above the water.

The funny thing about growing up is that you just assume that this kind of casual domestic violence is normal. It's the way dads are. It didn't make me a miserable child at all. I'd walk happily down the street in my short trousers and bow-tie, with a little quiff in my hair, dancing and singing as if I didn't have a care in the world. I'd get in from school at 3.30pm and play until five with the other kids in the neighbourhood. I remember my friend Gary, he had an Action Man. We'd run around playing action war games, dressing up as soldiers and thinking we were in the army too. Then I would come inside and have my tea. After that I'd do some drawing. I loved drawing. At bedtime I was given a milky drink and a biscuit. Life was not so bad after all.

Dad fancied himself as a bit of an entrepreneur and soon after we settled down in Wales my parents got into the guest-house business. Mum did a deal to buy a boarding house, but to bring in some money to pay for it they had to rent out their bungalow. We all had to move out of our home and live in a tiny caravan.

Mum and dad were making good money, but it didn't make mum happy. She was scared of my father and of what he might do to her and me. Even though she threatened to leave him, he thought she would never actually go. Apart from anything else, mum couldn't drive. Sometimes it just seemed impossible to get away.

The guest-house was huge. It had about 32 rooms and doing the housekeeping was like painting the Forth Bridge. It never seemed to end. I was only six but I had to do my bit. My job was to strip the beds and empty the bins every day. The north coast of Wales was a popular resort back then before foreign package tours took off, and the B&B was quickly successful. Every weekend throughout the summer, families would be leaving and others would be waiting to move into their rooms.

Things were such a success that my parents started to build up a bit of an empire on the coast. They soon opened up a cafe on the seafront. Dad ran the cafe like his own little military operation and once again everyone had to do their bit. I hated washing the dishes but I had to do it. He would make me butter 30 loaves of white bread in the morning before I went to school and another 30 in the afternoon when I got home. I wasn't allowed to play until the work had been done.

But there was another side to my father. He gave the orders but he didn't necessarily follow them himself. Mum would be working from seven in the morning until midnight and dad would be out womanising. I think mum realised that he had mistresses because he used to flaunt them in the town. I was the only one who didn't realise what was going on. He always wanted his independence. And mum couldn't argue with him. When my father made up his mind about something there was no room for negotiation.

Business boomed and they opened a second cafe near the local caravan park, where we took a caravan and lived for the season, freeing up the guest-house to take in more guests. On the park they would host talent nights. I think that was where I realised I liked being the centre of attention. Given half a chance I would be up on stage singing along to the music. I knew the words to all the songs because I'd heard them on the jukebox and because I was so small I would get a standing ovation at the end of each rendition. I loved the adulation.

It was fun being part of the holiday crowd. Dad also had an ice cream stall and Lorraine and I would help out. We'd offer to stand in for the girls so that they could go off for lunch and then we would pocket the money we made.

It was tough at home, but when I got away I had a great time. There were always new friends to make, kids down for the week on their holidays from Scotland and Liverpool. Mum would let me go off and play with them after I'd done my chores. Even if there wasn't anyone to play with I was happy to hang around the cafe. I'd sit around and wait for a customer to put some money in the jukebox. I can still remember the music that played on it – Puppet on a String, All You Need is Love, Neil Sedaka, Elvis Presley. I was always surrounded by music.

The cafe was right next to the funfair, and Lorraine and I soon learnt every scam in the book. We were like a couple of artful dodgers out of Oliver Twist, a right pair of urchins. At a very early age I learnt how to duck and dive, and it is a vital skill that has stood me in good stead ever since. If there was a dodgy way to make money I knew it. I could soon tell at a glance from the position of the wheels when the fruit machines were about to hit the jackpot. There were special places where you could hit other machines to make the money drop. I was only about seven and still small enough to squeeze behind the machines and pick up the loose change that had fallen down there, or even pick the locks and help myself to the cash inside the machines. We were feared by the people who ran the arcades – because my father had so much influence we got away with blue murder. It was from him that I had learnt how to bang fruit machines in the right place to get the money out. The owners would try to ban me from the arcades, but my dad would have a word with them and they'd have to let me back in. Having a business on the front was like being in the local Welsh mafia. The Taffia. You were all part of the same club, just a big, grown-up gang.

In the middle of every summer we would go off and have a holiday with mum's parents, brother and sisters in Blackwood, a mining village in south Wales. It's funny but everything was different down there, from the atmosphere to the ablutions. I remember that their toilet was in the back garden. Twice a week this tin bath would come out in front of the fire and my cousins and I would line up to get washed.

In some ways it felt more like home down south. I got more attention from my mum's parents, but I suppose that was because they didn't see me very often. I seemed to have a bigger, closer family there. I had lots of cousins: Mark, Shirley-Anne, Wayne and Lee. We used to play for hours in the park on the slides and swings and roundabouts. We didn't seem to have playgrounds like that back home, and I didn't want to go north again where dad would be waiting for me. As soon as I was back at the end of each summer I would start counting the days until I could visit them again. I'd be sad for ages. Nothing could cheer me up. Sometimes we would spend Christmas there too. It didn't matter how cold it was, we would be out playing until bedtime, something dad would never let me do.

Back in Kimmel Bay after the holidays there was always trouble looming in the shape of my father. Eventually, when I was nearly seven, mum decided she wanted to leave him. One day, when he was out, she took me and moved us into a top floor flat in Rhyl. I stayed off school for four days so that dad wouldn't be able to follow me home from the gates. Eventually I had to go back to school and as usual mum was right to have her suspicions. Dad found me, followed me home and pleaded with mum to give him another chance. She agreed to go back and he promised that he would change. But soon the same old problems of womanising and violence returned.

When I was seven, my sister Tanya was born. She was a lovely baby and because of the age gap I was able to look after her whenever mum was ill or had to pop out to the shops. I can remember one time Tanya started to cry as soon as mum went out. I tried everything to stop her from crying. I rocked her, carried her on my shoulder, walked her around the room. I was so worried in case I had hurt her in some way and made her cry. She just wouldn't stop. Maybe I'd been too rough when I picked her up, even though I was trying to be gentle. Maybe I had squeezed her too hard when I was hugging her. After about half an hour mum came back. Mum always knew what to do in these situations. But then again, it was simple. She was hungry. Mum gave her a bottle of milk and the crying stopped as quickly as it had started.

Mum loved Tanya and me, but her marriage to my dad was making her unhappy. I think Tanya's arrival hardened my mother's attitude. If Tanya's birth had changed my father she might have stayed with him, but it didn't seem to make any difference to him. Mum came to the conclusion that it would be better for Tanya and me if they split up. When Tanya was still a baby, mum arranged for Tanya to stay with her sister in Newbridge in south Wales and then mum told dad that she was going south as well. When he finally realised she meant it, he promised all sorts of things to get her to stay. He said he would buy her a car even though she had not passed her driving test. But it was too late. Mum took me, and we went to stay with her family in Newbridge.

South Wales meant freedom for all of us. No more beatings if I was five minutes late coming back from the funfair. I could go to the park and the swings, and stay out with other kids. My cousins were the same age as me, so even before I made new friends at school I had ready-made mates to play with. Mum came from a big, supportive family. Because she had been so young when I was born she actually had a brother who was younger than me. I must have been one of the few people able to boss his uncle about.

The strange thing about the divorce was that it seemed to happen overnight. I remember my mum telling me we were going to visit my grandparents. I just thought this was our usual summer holiday, leaving dad behind as usual to run the business. All I could think about was the fact that I would be free for another endless summer, that my dad wouldn't be there barking orders at me. When we arrived in Newbridge, the summer holiday was just like any summer holiday with my cousins. We unpacked our bags and set up home as always in Auntie Marion's house. She had a big house and mum, Tanya and I fitted into the attic, which was great because there was also a billiard table up there. It was only in September that my mum told us she had separated from my dad and that I would have to go to a new junior school. I thought I ought to be sad but I was happy to be away from my father. It felt as if a load had been lifted from my back. We were free. We could start a new life here without being told what we could and could not do.

It must have taken my mum a great deal of courage to leave my father. On the surface we seemed to have everything. Business was booming, Dad was making a good living from his cafe empire and extra work on the building site. We had a lovely big house with our very own swimming pool, but none of this could make up for the way my dad treated my mum. I think she was at the end of her tether. My parents split up just as my father was beginning to make a lot of money. He had a speedboat and was taking me for water-skiing lessons, but money wasn't everything. Mum just put her hands up and said she wanted out. I couldn't understand why. We had all this luxury and she didn't seem to want it. She just wanted a clean break so that she could start all over again.

Because we had left so quickly we had virtually nothing when we moved. Mum was always independent and determined to provide for us, so she went out to work and started badgering the council for a place of our own, while Auntie Marion and her husband, Mike, looked after Tanya and me. They also had a daughter of their own, my cousin Shirley-Anne. Things were a bit cramped at times, but I enjoyed living with her, and having a large family around me. When they were busy we were looked after by Uncle Mike's mother, Mrs Jones, an enigmatic, overweight old lady who would sit in the lounge with her legs apart. All I can remember about her is seeing her large bloomers whenever I stood in front of her.

I suppose deep down I knew that living in the attic couldn't last for ever, that it was only a temporary arrangement. But it was still a shock when we moved out into our own council house on a new housing estate on the outskirts of Newbridge, called, bizarrely, Pantside. We arrived on the estate on Christmas Eve. The house was right at the top of a big hill and the buses stopped halfway up. We had to walk the rest of the way. We didn't have any furniture, but we didn't care. We had our own home and our new life could begin. The next day was Christmas Day, but even though things were tight and mum had been really busy, she had saved up for our presents through local clubs. If she didn't have enough money she bought things from catalogues and made sure she paid the bill in the New Year. Mum made sure we never wanted for anything.

Things soon began to go decidedly downhill for my father. Mum passed her driving test and went up to Rhyl in a van to pick up our clothes. He was already struggling without her and it wasn't long before the money dried up. She had always been the brains behind his schemes and without her there he couldn't really cope. He tried to set up a new building business, but he couldn't manage that either and he soon went bankrupt. The flashy BMWs with the electric windows that used to impress the girls on the seafront were soon a thing of the past. The big house went too. He was back to where he started before he married mum.

We had to put the past behind us and begin our new lives. Mum always made sure I looked neat and tidy when I started at my new junior school. I got the nickname Man in a Suitcase after the television show at the time because I always used to carry my things in a briefcase.

At first I was a bit of a loner. I stood out because of my accent and it took me a while to make friends. Boys who had grown up in south Wales had very strong accents. Mine was not strong at all and it didn't help that I had a stubborn streak. Why should I change the way I speak? Sometimes I refused to change words into the Welsh equivalent. There was a boy in my class called Dai, for instance, which was the Welsh version of David. I always called him David, never Dai.

Instead of joining in with a gang I'd wander off into the mountains on my own. One day after a walk I turned up at home with a baby lamb, which I called Larry. 'Take him back, he needs his mother,' said mum. 'No, I'll look after him. I'll be his mother.' One of our neighbours had had quite a few children so I asked if I could have one of her spare feeding bottles. She gave me a bottle and I fed Larry three times a day, keeping him in the shed next to the coal-shed. I made him a little bed out of old blankets, but after a couple of weeks I realised things were getting out of hand. He was growing fast and sprouting horns. I came home one evening and I could hear him butting the shed door. Reluctantly I accepted that I had to let him go.

As I grew up and became more confident I always wanted to be the centre of attention. I think that was why I liked to dress up. When I was about ten I wanted to be a tap dancer, then I wanted to be a singer. I can remember singing Two Little Boys with the girls over the road. I even wrote to Hughie Green asking to go on Opportunity Knocks. I got a letter back from him saying he would let me know when he was doing auditions in the area, but I never heard from him again. I suppose being the oldest I had to learn to do a lot of things for myself. I was not the kind of boy who would hide away in his bedroom.

My mum was a big influence on me even before she split up with my dad, but maybe not having a father figure made her even more important. She was someone I could turn to. She was worried that I would miss out because my father wasn't around, but in fact I had a lot more freedom and to me that was much more important. Some of the things I was able to do I could never have done if my father had been there.

Mum was always more lenient, so once dad had gone I was able to stay out and play late without getting into trouble. Sometimes I did take advantage of mum. If I didn't feel like going to school I was able to fake an illness, pretend I had a stomach ache or a bad cold, and stay at home. Mum was a bit of an easy touch, but she was always important to me. Even today she is still one of the first people I'll go to if I have a problem.

My relationship with Tanya was a funny one. She looked up to me but that also meant that she wanted to hang around with me just at the time I wanted to be grown up and hang around with older mates.

Eventually I'd had enough of it. One day when she was about four mum left me to look after her when I wanted to go out to the park. I locked her in the coal-shed at the bottom of the garden until I came back. I opened the door and said 'Tanya, can you just get that sack for me from the back of the shed?' As soon as she was in I closed the door. I opened the door three hours later and she was covered in coal dust and dirt. I told her, 'If you tell mum what I've done you'll never be able to play with me again.' Of course, I loved and cared about Tanya, and would never have let her come to any real harm. I was her big brother and, with Dad gone, her protector too. But I was 11 years old and wanted to be with my mates; I didn't want a four-year-old girl tagging along.

I was always mean to Tanya. While I was babysitting, I'd play cards with her for money, but she had no idea how to play. Mum would come home and make me give back all the money I had won, but I didn't care. As soon as mum was back I was able to go out and see my mates. When I was left with Tanya to do the chores I would make her do the housework and if it wasn't good enough I'd lock her in the shed. It was almost as if I was repeating the behaviour of my dad, except that I was only joking. We would argue over everything. I suppose there was a bit of tension because until she came along I had had mum to myself. We always fought over crisps and biscuits until in the end mum gave us our own supplies which we kept in our own tins in our own cupboards.

But if anyone else picked on Tanya they had me to answer to. I always stood up for her. It was a rough estate and you had to be strong to survive. It was our valley fighting against the gang from the next valley. If I had to fight I would. This was the land of miners and rugby players. I had no choice but to learn to look after myself. But there was another happy side to growing up. I used to pretend I was in the Olympics. There was a whole gang of us: Neil, Keith and Michael Mathews, Jeremy Shepherd. And also girls like Sally Blanche and Lorraine, Angela and Maria Castri. We would make up teams and run the 100 metres and do the long jump, and I'd imagine I'd won the gold medal. Or we would get together and have our own Wimbledon tournament, marking out a tennis court on the road with chalk. In our minds it was the real thing.

I eased comfortably into my new life. I found school quite easy, even though I was often working hard at the weekends, earning money for clothes. Those early mornings in the cafe, rising at dawn to butter endless mountains of bread had taught me to combine work with play. Those extra hours awake made me feel as if I was living two lives while the other children were only living one. I never seemed to get tired, I was always busy. Once we had settled in Newbridge I started to see my father again, travelling up to stay with him. I'd spend my afternoons hanging around on the seafront, just like in the old days. If the weather wasn't any good I'd go and play bingo, using some of the inside knowledge my dad had taught me. There were certain seats where you could sit and almost be guaranteed a win because the boards that lit up had the right numbers on them. Some boards could never win because they were missing certain numbers. Every time you won a game you collected a prize voucher. You could use these vouchers on the stall if you fancied a teddy bear or a bucket, but it just so happened that you could also use them in Mr Paul's, the only decent clothes shop in Rhyl. I was about 11 and just starting to get into fashion. All the trendy people in the area went there and you could get anything there from Ben Sherman shirts to Sta-Prest trousers. You couldn't do it every day, but every few days I'd go back and win a few more games. It took a lot of bingo to win enough vouchers for a pair of trousers, but it was worth it. It was not exactly designer fashions but it was the best shop around, the first in the town to get the latest clothes in from London. North Wales was a brilliant place for picking up new clothes. Fashions seemed to reach there from London before they reached south Wales. I'd go with an empty case and return with a full one. Down south I was the king because I was wearing the latest trend.

I felt great. I looked like a proper little skinhead. It made people think that I was always ready for a fight, but I was actually into the skinhead look rather than the aggressive attitude. A lot of skinheads went to Cardiff City's football matches, so I went along, but when I realised they were going along for a fight, I stopped. I was wearing the clothes because I was into the style, not because I was into violence. It was around this time that I really started getting interested in style. From the age of about 12 I *had* to be the trendiest kid on the block.

Money was tight, but then I had a stroke of luck. Robert Barker, the owner of the best clothes shop in Blackwood, noticed that I was interested in clothes and we got chatting. Eventually he offered me a Saturday job. I'd spend every weekend working there. As soon as I was paid I went straight back into the shop and spent the money on clothes. I'd walk down the street wearing 22-hole Dr Martens, baggy baker boy pants in either denim or pure white, then a white cardigan with two blue stripes, then a checked tam-o'-shanter with a bobble on the top. It was the look that teenagers wore before the Bay City Rollers adapted it.

It's funny the things you inherit from your parents – just like my father I wouldn't go out of the house until the creases on my trousers were exactly right. It was important to get the look absolutely right – my top pocket had to have a silk hankie sticking out, even though it was only a triangle of silk stapled to a piece of cardboard that was hidden inside the pocket.

The following summer I went back to stay with my father for a second time. It was only now that I was a little older that I realised what he was really like. He had an eye for the ladies and didn't want the fact that he had children to cramp his style. When we were out on the seafront he told me that if he got talking to any potential conquests I should say that I was his younger brother. We'd go water-skiing and the women would come and watch us. It seemed harmless enough at the time, and it even made me feel quite grown up, part of an adult game. But there was another side to my father which made me feel sorry for my mother.

One night I was staying at his house and found out what had finally driven her away from the man that she had once loved. I knew he had occasionally hit and slapped my mum but I had never seen anything like this. I was asleep on the sofa when I heard a woman screaming. I thought that maybe I was dreaming but, rubbing my eyes, I realised I was not seeing things. My father was dragging his girlfriend Blanche around the room by her long blonde hair and kicking the shit out of her while she was whimpering and crying. When he saw me watching he just shouted, 'Get back to your fucking bedroom, this has nothing to do with you.'

I wanted to help her but I couldn't. In the morning I saw her again. Her face was black and blue and the first thing she said to me was, 'Tell your dad's parents it was an accident. I fell down the stairs.' After that incident I vowed I would not go and stay with my father ever again. Mum remembers me coming back home and not talking about the visit, but she didn't realise why I was suddenly so withdrawn. But after that, whenever dad came south to pick up Tanya for the weekend I would always run off so that he couldn't persuade me to go back with him. I didn't want anything to do with him after what I saw that night.

CHAPTER TWO

THE VILLAGE FREAK

In the summer of 1970 I had passed my eleven-plus and started at Newbridge Grammar School. It was a good school, but things were changing in the education system. Grammar schools were being abolished everywhere because they were perceived as bastions of privilege. In Newbridge though, the grammar school gave working-class kids the chance to better themselves. It gave young boys from mining families an opportunity to do well enough to go to university, maybe go on to become a doctor or a lawyer rather than go down the pits as their fathers and grandfathers had done before them. Without those schools, a Welsh working-class lad back in the seventies had two possible career options: the mines or the rugby field. Neither of which appealed to me.

The following year Newbridge Grammar School became comprehensive and merged with the local secondary school to become Greenfield Comprehensive. I liked fitting in and being part of a gang, but I found that I liked standing out even more. I now realised that I had always wanted to be different from other people. Gradually I started to make myself look not just fashionable, but unique. My classic skinhead look was evolving into something more distinctive. Everyone at school had to wear the same all-black uniform so the best way of expressing my individuality was through my hairstyle. I had stood out at the end of junior school because of my skinhead crew cut, but I was growing that out now and experimenting with longer hair.

My accent didn't stick out as much as when I had first arrived, but the merging of the schools meant that there was a bit of rivalry between the different groups. There was still a bit of an initiation ceremony to go through before I could be completely accepted as one of the lads. One day I was challenged to a fight by one of the bigger boys. Everyone expected me to be beaten to a pulp, but I won. Maybe it was my father's influence, wanting to make a man of me, but I could always handle myself.

Winning was a bit of a problem too because it then meant that everyone else wanted to fight me. But it did establish me as part of the local gang and we started to get together after school. The Pantside estate wasn't finished, so the building site was our play area. We used half-assembled houses as our climbing frames, played hide and seek under the floorboards and leapt across the half-built foundations pretending to be pirates – the kind of dangerous games that would never be allowed nowadays.

I'd stopped listening to my mum's records and had started to develop my own tastes in music. The natural role model was David Bowie. He was a big star but different to your average pop singer. I liked Marc Bolan and Bryan Ferry, but Bowie was the best. By the summer of 1973 he was at his commercial peak, having already topped the album charts with Aladdin Sane earlier in the year. I had his posters all over my wall. He seemed to be perfect. He had a great look and made great music. I admired the way he was able to reinvent himself with a new look for each album.

He made me want to form a band as well as look like him. I had some good friends by now. People like Keith Williams, Michael Williams, Steven Davey and Kim Walker. Following in the footsteps of David Bowie, I tried to get a band going. I got Michael Hawker on drums, Paul Beach on bass and another local lad on lead guitar. But it didn't last very long. Everyone was too busy doing other stuff to concentrate on it. We'd try to get together to have a band practice and there would always be somebody off playing football. Mum encouraged me by paying for me to have guitar lessons, but I couldn't get the hang of it because I was left-handed and my guitar tutor was right-handed.

It seemed that the only way I could successfully emulate David

Bowie was by copying his hair. It was pretty unusual for a boy to dye his hair back in those days, but as David Bowie unveiled each new look I had to be the first one in Newbridge to copy him. After me, everybody started to model themselves on David Bowie. In September 1973 David Bowie's album of cover versions, Pin Ups, was released. I remember going to the local record store in Pontypool on the day it came out and queuing up before the shop even opened. I'd heard that they were only going to stock three copies and I had to make sure I got one before they all sold out.

During that time my mum's kitchen became a regular social focal point for my friends. My mum's sister Glenys was a hairdresser so I had access to all the latest hair colour products. Because she was out at work all day, mum didn't know anything at all about this, until one afternoon she came back home early and had the shock of her life. Four boys from Greenfield Comprehensive were in her kitchen having their hair highlighted. I think it was only then that I really started to be outwardly creative. That was when I started to rebel more than ever in terms of my appearance.

I suppose I met up with my first real girlfriend Cherie Beasant when I was into David Bowie. We became known as the 'village freaks' because we looked so different from everybody else, but the same as each other. We both thought Bowie was a god and had our hair cut in the spiky, bog-brush style. And when we both dyed our hair orange, we were banned from school. I thought, 'Great, I'm off school for three weeks.' My mum stood by me, she went into the school and spoke to the headmaster, 'I don't understand how having bright orange hair is going to affect his education.' But he refused to let me return until I dyed it black again. I got my revenge though. After a while I streaked my hair blond, which was just about allowed, and came up with a way of re-making the regulation all-black Greenfield Comp uniform. I wore really baggy trousers while everyone else wore straight trousers. Instead of a V-neck jumper I wore a twin set, a jumper with no sleeves and a cardigan. It was the kind of thing a girl would wear, but I wasn't trying to dress like a girl, I was just trying to dress differently to all the other boys.

Gradually my lifestyle also had a dramatic effect on my academic progress. Until this point I had been a grade A student in everything. But suddenly in the fourth year I was put down into Class C. During my David Bowie phase I had been happy to go to school when they let me, but as I reached my early teens I started to mix with older boys and I became more interested in northern soul. I was going out in the evening clubbing for the first time and this was affecting my studies a lot more than dyeing my hair ever did.

The place that did the most damage was Wigan Casino, the legendary northern soul club in north-west England, about 200 miles from Newbridge. Once I got into northern soul, Wigan became the centre of my life and I started growing away from my classmates and hanging about with older mates who were into it, people like Jethro and Kim from Wolverhampton, Steve Jones from Blackwood, Noddy and Sparky from Oakdale. I was into everything about it: the clothes, the dancing, the travelling. It was the first place that I had a sexual experience with girls, although, unlike local clubs it was a place you went to for the music, not the opposite sex. Fans were obsessed by the records, prepared to pay up to £500 for an old seven-inch single by an obscure American artist who had never had a sniff of Top of the Pops. Edwin Starr had only had a couple of small hits but he was about the biggest name ever to come out of the northern soul scene. Gloria Jones recorded Tainted Love, which was only a cult club hit until Soft Cell covered it in the early eighties.

The clothes were particularly important. The shoes had to be leather-soled so that you could slide across the dance-floor and do your backdrops and splits. The main move that took a bit of practice, involved kicking your legs in the air and falling back on to your hands. I watched Jethro do it and practised at home in my bedroom until I knew I could get it right in public.

Because Wigan was so far away it took quite a bit of organising to get up there every weekend. I worked Friday nights after school as an apprentice at the butcher's counter in Tescos and sometimes on Saturday mornings too to pay for the trips. The job had its lighter moments. One day I came home from work at the butcher's with a pig's eye and pretended it was a human one just to tease Tanya.

Once I had finished work on Saturdays I'd pick up my Adidas sports bag that I had already packed and I'd be off. My mum worried about me falling in with an older crowd and some weekends, if I was at home, she would try to stop me from going by shutting me in the bathroom because it was the only room in the house with a lock. But I'd climb out of the window, get down a drainpipe and hitchhike. If I was lucky I'd get a lift all the way to Manchester, and from there it was a short bus ride to Wigan. Other times I'd get to Wolverhampton and join a coach party there. By hook or by crook I would get to Wigan.

Some weekends were epic affairs taking in a number of different clubs around England. There might be a coach to Blackpool Mecca, which opened at around 10pm and closed at about 1am, then another coach would go on to Wigan which would open at 2am and continue until 10am the following Sunday morning. From there we'd go off to the swimming pool to freshen up, ready for more dance-floor action. Then we would go to an all-dayer before returning to Newbridge overnight. Other times I'd sling my bag with its Keep The Faith stickers over my shoulder and head for the Spinning Wheel or the Torch in Manchester, Samantha's in Sheffield or south to Bristol.

Clubbing was more about dancing than sex, but I did find the time to lose my virginity. Steve Jones wanted to go out with a girl called Heather, but she was always hanging around with her best mate, Angie, so he thought the best way to work things out would be if I made up a foursome. One weekend Steve's parents were away and he invited these two girls back. I ended up with Angie. It all happened very quickly and I didn't think any more about it. It was a few years later, when I found out that she had had to have an abortion, that it did have an effect on me, thinking that I'd fathered a baby that was so quickly disposed of.

Maybe my mum was right to be concerned about me. It was at this time that I started to dabble with drugs. The clubs used to be open all night but they didn't sell alcohol. About 80 per cent of the people there were speed freaks. You needed to take drugs to keep going for so long and there was always somebody hanging around who could supply

you with what you needed. The amphetamines were normally prescribed for women to help them lose weight. They stopped your appetite and also kept you awake. They all had nicknames: blues, black
bombers, green and clears, brown and clears . . .

We would take anything to keep us up all night. I'd stay awake for
48 hours then I'd get back to Wales on the Monday morning and go
straight into school. I don't know what was worse, the come-down
after the drugs wore off or trying to concentrate on the blackboard
while I was still speeding. Either way I'd be sitting at the back of the
class like a zombie, oblivious to everything that was going on around
me.

And yet I don't think the teachers even knew what I was up to. All
they knew was that I was not doing as well as I had been doing. Nor
were a lot of the other pupils. I didn't brag about it; I thought the
others at school were more immature than me and had different
interests and we simply grew apart. I just went off school because I
was away doing my own thing with a grown-up crowd. School didn't
seem relevant any more. I only paid attention to my art classes and my
art teacher, Mr Gwynn. He showed more interest in my work than the
other teachers and he prompted me to put together a portfolio of my
work, which would pay off in later years when I showed my sketches
to The Sex Pistols and Generation X, and they employed me to come
up with design ideas for them.

My attendance record plummeted. My mum went to work on the
9am bus, while my school bus went at 8.30am, so instead of getting on
it I'd hide in a field until mum had gone to work. I had keys to the
house so as soon as the coast was clear I went back home and took all
the other boys who were bunking off school with me.

When the teachers saw how badly I was doing, they spoke to my
mum about me. They said I was being silly because I was a bright
student with great prospects. None of them really seemed that interested in my future though. The only real support I got was from my
art teacher. I made sure that however tired I was I always completed
my art portfolio. I'm not knocking education, but I thought that I was
going to have a career doing something connected to art, so I felt that

that was all that I needed. I didn't ever think I'd be working in an office.

It was during my northern soul days, and about a year after I had started going to Wigan Casino that I had my first run-in with the police. One night mum had a message to call the police station in Cannock, near Wolverhampton. I had been caught after breaking into a pharmacy. I was the youngest and smallest of the group, so the others had sent me through the back window to steal the pills which were kept in the dangerous drugs cabinet. Unfortunately somebody had handed my description to the police and as I was walking along later that night an unmarked police car screeched to a halt and a hand hoiked me into the back, saying, 'You're the little bastard who has been breaking into all of these chemists.' It was only once I was in the car that I found out they were plain-clothed officers from the drug squad.

I thought I was good at pulling the wool over people's eyes. I had once tried to get into the cinema to see The Exorcist when I was under age, and when I was turned away I went to a phone box, called the cinema, pretended to be the manager and said one of my employees had been turned away. Then I went back and got in. I thought I could get away with anything, but the Wolverhampton police were too clever. I'd been cocky, saying they had the wrong person, but I was taken to the station where I denied the charges. They obviously knew it was me. They looked in my sports bag and underneath the bit of stiffened cardboard at the bottom they found a couple of pills which had iden-tifying numbers on them to trace them back to the chemist's that had been broken into. I couldn't really deny it any longer.

When the police found out that I was only 14 and still a juvenile they contacted my mother to come to get me. I was so scared. I just wanted to go home to my mum. But it wasn't quite as simple as that. She didn't have a car at the time so she called my father and asked him to pick me up. Not surprisingly his attitude to my crime was much tougher. He didn't want to know. The only other members of the family who had a car were mum's parents and she didn't want my nan to know what had happened to me, so she had to tell the police to put me in the local boys' home until the case came to court a fortnight later. Those weeks were awful. And what made it even worse was that just as that fortnight was up, the court case was postponed and I was sent back to the home for another week. Mum could probably have come up sooner and brought me home by bus, but I think she was at the end of her tether by then and wanted to teach me a lesson. My father certainly wanted the punishment to be severe in the hope that it might drum some sense into me.

To say that borstal was very much a learning experience is an understatement. My dad might have been strict with me, but this regime came as a real wake-up call to the system. The idea was that this short sharp shock would leave its mark and make sure the inmates didn't get up to anything like this again. Of course, a lot of the kids were destined for a life of crime. For many, borstal was little more than a brutal university of criminality and many would graduate with honours. What really scared me though was that the grown men in uniform weren't the ones in control.

The guards imposed the strict discipline and made us do daily cross-country runs, stand to attention and get back to our dormitories for lights out. But as soon as you got there you realised that it wasn't the guards that you had to worry about. The older boys who had seen it all before ruled the roost. You had to watch yourself all the time. It was frightening at night in the dorms. Anything could happen. They used bully boy tactics, such as coming up behind you and throwing a blanket over your head. If you grassed on somebody you would always get a beating. There was lots of gay activity going on, but I didn't have a clue about what being gay was then. I was glad to be out of there when the day came to appear in court. Maybe until then I'd been a jack-the-lad who thought he could get away with anything, but those three weeks knocked the stuffing out of me. It really shook me up. I was very lucky though. I got off with a caution as it was my first offence, but worse than that was the telling off from my mother. She banned me from going to Wigan ever again. I wouldn't be climbing down any more drainpipes for a while.

I may have stopped staying out all weekend, but I had got the clubbing bug and instead I started investigating a scene that was much closer to home. By late 1975 we were all dyeing our hair. I was hardly ever at school now, so it didn't seem to matter if I got expelled. I can remember watching John Hurt in The Naked Civil Servant and it fascinated me – partly because of his dyed orange hair, but also because he was gay. I'd never really thought that I might be gay or bisexual before – up until now I'd always had girlfriends – but this made me think about things like that. Quentin Crisp became one of my all-time heroes. I liked him for his eccentricity. He had an awful lot of guts to walk around the way he did in those days. My mum was quite shocked by the programme. When she came into the lounge she made me change channels, but as soon as she went out again I changed back.

It turned out that there was a pretty vibrant creative club scene virtually on my doorstep in Newport and Cardiff. There was something about Newport and the surrounding area that made it stylish and fashion conscious. By the summer of 1976 we had started to wear Fiorucci see-through plastic macs with bright, pegged trousers and mohair jumpers. When we were meeting up in Newport or Cardiff I had to leave early and I would always get strange looks at the bus stop. But once the bus pulled into Cwmbran I knew I'd be joined by other people, such as Josie and Jill, and that helped me to relax. By the time we got to Newport there would be a regular group together: me, Colin Fisher, Mark Stephenson, Noddy, Bob Channing, Mark Taylor, Jonathan James, Steven Mahoney, Chris Sullivan.

We were a real gang and were always getting into scrapes. Jonathan James was the only person among us who had a telephone because his dad was the local funeral director in nearby Aberfan. I'd rung Jonathan one night and we had arranged to meet Chris Sullivan in Newport. I'd heard about this great army surplus store which sold PVC and plastic clothes, which we were really into ripping up and customising. Having done our shopping we were walking back to the bus station to go home when Chris decided that he was having a hunger attack and that he would catch us up at the bus stop. Jonathan and I continued to walk along slowly while Chris went into Marks and Spencers. We were just beginning to wonder what had happened to Chris, when suddenly this figure came bounding down the street, pushing people out of the way and shouting, 'Leg it, I've been caught!' We ran for the bus station and jumped on a bus that was about to pull out. Chris had been trying to nick something in the shop and had sent a woman flying as he ran out. It turned out that the bus we were on went to Newbridge and not Merthyr where they lived, but we all went back to my house and my mum, being the soft touch that she was, gave them a lift home, not knowing what Chris had been up to.

We took a lot of stick for our appearance. At night we would constantly end up in bloody fights with the local piss-heads. This was a place where it was considered effeminate to wear deodorant, so a man in make-up was asking for trouble. But whatever we looked like we were still valley boys and we knew how to look after ourselves. One night we were chased down Newport High Street. We got cornered, but we gave as good as we got. Sometimes there was tension with crowds from Bristol who thought they were better than us, but eventually we became one big group. We were all on the same side against the grey, ordinary people with their boring, drab nine-to-five lives.

Newport kids were already sporting wedge haircuts and becoming soul boys and while Wigan was out of bounds for me, London wasn't. I heard about clubs in the capital where kids dressed like us and I started making trips to places like the Lacy Lady in Ilford and the Global Village underneath the arches at Charing Cross. It was in places like this that I first saw the punk thing happening long before the press picked up on it. People like Siouxsie Sioux and Billy Idol would be hanging around and I'd see how they were being creative and not just wearing clothes they had bought in the high street chain stores. I also saw the clothes in shops in the King's Road, such as Acme Attractions and Sex, which were unlike anything I had ever seen before. Punk seemed to be the most exciting thing in years. I was desperate to be a part of it.

Back in Wales I started putting my own outfits together, wearing plastic bin bags and ripping up clothes and safety pinning them back together. I dyed my hair jet black and made it stand up in spikes. Word soon got around about my appearance. The *Western Mail* ran an article with the headline 'Hey punks, meet the chain gang' and said I was the first punk in Wales. There was a photo of me in my black plastic jumpsuit with my eyes heavily made up, my nose pierced and three chains from my nose to my left ear. The feature talked about this outrageous new cult and quoted me as saying that the only thing that worried my mum 'is the neighbours'.

Luckily mum was away on holiday in Jersey when the paper came out, but my auntie met her at the station with the words, 'Well, Gill, your son has finally made the papers.' My mum just groaned and replied, 'What has he been up to now?' I think she was used to my antics by this time. When she got home and walked into the bedroom I was busy ripping up my shirts and putting emulsion stripes on my trousers. The room smelt like a paint factory.

Punk rock was a new rallying flag around which anyone who was different could gather. And the meeting place for this new clan seemed to be my mum's house. Whenever she was away we would have parties. Everyone would gather in the house before we all trooped off to a club. In a way I was getting people to go to clubs just the same as I would be doing five years later, except I wasn't making any money out of it. As everyone converged on the estate, there would be girls tottering along the street in high heels and fishnet stockings, with hair all colours of the rainbow and beyond. I remember neighbours saying it was as if martians had invaded Pantside.

Soon people were coming to Newport from as far as Bristol because they had heard that something exciting and new was going on there. Once, when mum was away for a fortnight, I knew the house would be empty so I invited everyone from the club in Newport back to Newbridge. There were girls with beehive hairdos in gold stilettos, mini-skirts, boob tubes and see-through plastic macs walking in and out of the house. When mum came back the neighbours told my mum I'd been making porno movies. I suppose that element of me being an entrepreneur stemmed from the love of wanting to be involved in the music. I just wanted to be at the heart of it.

The moment we had all been waiting for was when The Sex Pistols came to perform at the Stowaway Club in Newport in September 1976.

What I remember most is when the curtains opened and they saw the audience. There was already a big punk scene in Newport and the band was actually surprised at how outrageous we were. I can actually say that I shocked The Sex Pistols, which is an unusual achievement.

The Sex Pistols had the biggest effect on me. I saw those four lads and thought that anyone could get up onstage and be in a band. Seeing them made me decide I wanted to have another go at being in a band. They were saying 'we can't play', and neither could I, but now it didn't matter. They just seemed like the perfect answer to the bland disco music that had taken over the charts, stuff like Chic and Donna Summer. I remember Carwash, it was a hit and the title of a movie, but I couldn't help thinking how colourless it was compared to the explosive energy of punk.

After the gig I hung around to meet the band. Johnny Rotten was his typically off-ish self but I struck up a friendship with the bass player Glen Matlock. He was very supportive and gave me his phone number. We talked every week on the phone even though this meant that I had to walk down to the phone box about a mile away at the bottom of the hill because we didn't have a phone in the house. The Sex Pistols were like a drug. Once you had experienced them you were hooked.

By now I was determined to get out of Newbridge permanently. I knew there was something else going on in the world and I wanted to be a part of it. But before I could leave I started to put on bands around south Wales. I wanted to get the punk message across. I did everything. I organised and booked the club and did the artwork for the posters which I then had to spend all day sticking up around the town.

Punk bands were having difficulty getting gigs so they were happy to come down to play to an appreciative crowd in south Wales. I put on gigs by Generation X, The Stranglers and eventually The Sex Pistols themselves. It was not easy setting them up without a phone in the house. I had to walk up and down that hill in all sorts of weather, in the heaviest snow and the wettest rain, to arrange things. But it was worth it. I got to know Billy Idol of Generation X and Glen Matlock very well. They both realised how desperate I was to get out of south Wales and promised to help me out if I ever came to London.

The local gig by The Stranglers sticks in my mind because that was when I had my first homosexual experience. They weren't a huge band back then but they were building up a loyal cult following for their cross between pub rock, punk rock and aggressive R&B. I'd never really had any sex education. My mum had never talked to me about sex. I had just had a snog with Cherie Beasant, that one-night stand with Angie at Steve Jones's house and a few messy casual encounters at Wigan Casino. There had been one girl called Laura, but it was a very quick thing in a Wigan shop doorway, over in a matter of minutes with both of us not really knowing what we were doing. It was not what I expected.

Looking back on it now, Jean-Jacques Burnel, the band's bass player, basically initiated me. I suppose he would have been in his mid-twenties at the time and I was a teenager, very star struck and he was the stud of the band. After the gig at the Roundabout Club in Newport he asked me where I lived. He left the band and paid for a taxi back to my house about 15 miles away. I was very drunk and it was really late and I was just hoping that my mum wasn't going to wake up. At that age I didn't really know what was going to happen, but I think maybe I've always had the kind of personality that wants to try everything at least once.

As we stumbled in, my mum appeared in the hall and asked what was going on. Luckily she did not think anything was out of the ordinary. As we clattered up the stairs to my bedroom, trying not to wake Tanya, she just thought he was a friend who needed a bed for the night. And by this time I'd taken it upon myself to put a lock on my bedroom door. Not because I was bringing people back all the time but because I would often spend my evenings in there ripping up my clothes and spraying them with paint, and I didn't want to be disturbed. Mum had been surprised enough when she caught me dyeing my hair. Every time she smelt paint she wondered what I was up to. One evening she came in and caught me cutting up my clothes. She was furious and told me to stop immediately. So the first thing I did on the night that Jean-Jacques came back was make sure that once we were inside my room I put the padlock on the door. It was the first time that I had kissed a man passionately, and sexually it opened my eyes, though not completely. I still didn't know what gay was, let alone bisexual. In some ways it just confused me even more. I wanted to be with women and I also wanted to be with men. What did that make me?

The morning after was a pretty strange affair. Jean-Jacques had to get home and it was only then in the sober light of day that he realised exactly how far he was from the nearest train station. He had spent all of his money on the cab the previous night and had to hitch back to London. I remember getting on the bus with him to show him where to hitch from and saying goodbye to him on the edge of the motorway.

I guess it was a one-night stand, but Jean-Jacques was very friendly, suggesting that I should look him up if I ever came to London. Maybe he thought I would never make the move, but gradually I was building up the courage to leave Wales. I was becoming obsessed with the idea; I just needed that extra push. Every time I had some contact with a London band they recommended that I moved to the capital. When I put Billy Idol's new band Generation X on, Billy showed a lot of interest in the artwork I had done to advertise the gigs. He was very impressed and said that if I ever moved up to London, once they got a record contract there would be a job for me.

By this time there was no point me staying on at school. I had outgrown the boys in my class and was moving in a completely differ-ent world. I needed to get out of Newbridge fast. I was lucky that I now had some contacts in London. My mother was worried because London seemed such a different world to south Wales, but I knew that it was a world where I belonged. I wouldn't have much money but I would get by. Jean-Jacques Burnel had also said he would put me up. We didn't ever have a sexual encounter again, but he let me stay on his sofa when I came up to London.

Life was beginning to open up for me. It was the end of one period and the dawning of a new age. Another dramatic thing also happened that helped me to draw a line under the past. My father died. I got a message about it when I was working part-time at the butcher's department in Tescos. He had had a brain tumour. I don't know if he had ever got over my mother leaving him. I went to the funeral. I was the only one who didn't cry. I knew what he had put my mum through.

CHAPTER THREE
CLUBLAND

In November 1976 I finally made the move to London. I set off on the train to Paddington with £30 in my pocket and a couple of offers of temporary accommodation. Glen Matlock had said I could always come up and sleep on his sofa and I jumped at the chance. I stayed at Glen's flat in Maida Vale for a few nights before moving in with a couple of Welsh girls, Sandra Kinrade and Jo Cheetah, who were living at their auntie's house near the Oval cricket ground in south London.

I couldn't have timed my arrival in London better. Things were really beginning to take off for The Sex Pistols and you could just sense that the whole punk scene was about to explode. It was just what the country needed. The band's début single, Anarchy in the UK, had just been released and they were getting ready to go on tour. There was just the small matter of a bit of television promotion, appearing on Thames Television's Today programme with veteran journalist Bill Grundy. The performance would put them and punk rock on the front page of every newspaper in the country.

As soon as I got to London I got completely wrapped up in the punk scene. Everything was happening so fast. The press generated this rivalry between punks and teddy boys and I was beaten up a couple of times around the Oval. But it was all part of life back then. You took it in your stride. It was no big deal as long as you had a few pounds in your pocket and a gig to go to that night.

The early punk scene was an exciting time. Gradually a group of us built up that would go to gigs together: Jo and Sandra, and my new friends Mark and Wendy May, who lived out of town in Borehamwood.

I had a brief relationship with Wendy which had its exciting moments. We were travelling back to Borehamwood one night when we decided to have sex on the train. I was quite nervous, but we were on an old style train with no corridors between the carriages. You could only get in from the outside, and Wendy said, 'Don't worry, the train doesn't stop at another station for half an hour.' Of course, it did, and we had to make ourselves decent quickly as the train pulled in.

We started to hang out at Louise's, the lesbian club in Poland Street, that was also an early punk hangout. It was there that I got to know the south London gang known as the Bromley Contingent, which included Siouxsie of the Banshees and Billy Idol. We'd also go to the Global Village, the disco under the arches at Charing Cross, which later became Heaven. This was a strange club where I'd first noticed the evolution of punk fashion. Soul boys and girls with flicks and wedges started to evolve into punks with safety pins and plastic bags. It was the main place in London where young people who were not just into music, but also the way they looked and expressed themselves, could go and not feel people were staring at them for the wrong reasons. Later on, things became more difficult. We would go to venues like the Hope and Anchor in Islington and the Man in the Moon in the King's Road. Fights would often break out. Saturday afternoons down the King's Road felt like West Side Story, only less kitsch, more heavy. Of course, it wasn't all punk rock glamour. I never expected the streets to be paved with gold, but sometimes it was much harder than I thought it would be. There were times when I was on death's door. It was hard living on £11 a week dole money, and unsettled too, moving from sofa to sofa, from squat to squat. It was only really one step up from being homeless. Some of the places I stayed in had no hot water and I had to go to the swimming baths to get clean.

I was not eating much either, partly through lack of money, partly because taking speed meant that I didn't have much of an appetite. My bondage trousers were five sizes too big. The way I had to pull them in at the waist made it look as if I was trying to start a new fashion. I changed my image like other people changed their socks. One week I'd have black hair and a leather jacket, the next week I'd be wearing a peaked army cap. But I soon had a regular look sorted out. The arms of my shirts were held together by safety pins, my jumpers had holes in them and I used to adore my full-length, leather SS army coat. My crowning glory though was my hair. I dyed it pure white and, with hairspray, made it stick out as much as possible, shaping it into spikes with the aid of KY jelly. At the time it seemed like an original style, but as the months drew on and other people copied me it began to feel as if the look was a uniform you could pick up from your high street.

No sooner had I arrived than The Sex Pistols set off on the infamous Anarchy Tour, or at least what was left of it after so many dates had been cancelled. I couldn't get enough of them and started following them to the gigs. If I couldn't get a lift with them I'd hitch to Portsmouth or the north of England and even up to Scotland just to catch another show. I remember in Portsmouth somebody in the audience was trying to get everybody who wasn't a punk to riot, they were all shouting, 'You're shit, you're crap.' This huge fight broke out and the punks came off better.

One of the few remaining shows was in Caerphilly. I remember it well because first of all I went back to Newbridge to meet my friends and we all travelled up together. When we got there, people from the local church were protesting outside the gig, saying that The Sex Pistols were evil. A vicar was shouting through a loudspeaker that Satan would enter the body of anyone who went in to see this vile band. It was just in the run-up to Christmas, and there were Welsh carol singers there too. People were blessing us and throwing holy water over us as we went in.

Sometimes I was able to cadge a lift on the tour bus. I struck up a friendship with Johnny Thunders and Walter Lure from the American support band, the Heartbreakers, and their manager, Leee Black Childers. Leee's secretary was a fascinating figure called Gayle, a larger-than-life lady with peroxide yellowish blonde hair, who talked in a real American drawl. I was still very naive about gays, but Leee always had these pretty boys with him and I was always invited to parties at his house. At the time, it must have been the end of 1976, The Heartbreakers were living in Sydney Street in Chelsea and the parties there used to be pretty debauched. Through The Heartbreakers I met people like Debbie Harry and Joan Jett, who became regulars at Chelsea parties when they were in London. But there was a darker side to this 24-hour hedonism too. It was at the Sydney Street flat that I first saw people injecting drugs. While the drug of choice on the London punk circuit had been speed, the American punks had introduced heroin into the scene. At The Heartbreakers' house, I walked into a room and saw someone injecting heroin. I thought I knew all about drugs but this was horrible. It put me off needles for life.

Even though I had been to bed with one man, London's sophisticated gay culture was a complete mystery to me. One night I went out with my friend Chris. My hair was bleached into a pure white quiff, I was wearing my red PVC Seditionaries trousers with these zips at the back which, if you left them open, would show your arse. And I had the infamous 'cowboys' T-shirt with the two cowboys in leather with their cocks sticking out. We went into a pub for a pint and these men were suddenly like bees around a honey pot. They looked like a mixture of fitness instructors and leather bikers. I thought we were going to get our heads kicked in, but what I didn't realise was that we were like nectar to them. I said we had better finish our drinks and get out. As we were leaving these four guys tried to get us to stay by blocking the doorway. We said 'excuse me' and walked out as fast as we could. As I left, I looked back and saw these two big, burly guys kissing each other. That was my first experience of going into a gay bar, which shows just how naive I was. I thought it was an ordinary pub, but it was actually the Coleherne, one of the most famous heavy gay leather pubs in Earl's Court.

Life in London was just what I had been longing for all my life. Gigs every night, hanging out with like-minded people during the day, no one to tell you what you had to wear, and no one was the odd one out. I finally fitted in. Everyone seemed to be an exhibitionist like me. Even now, after everything that I have gone through, I still love London.

It was while I was staying at Jean-Jacques' place that I became involved with a girl called Suzi. She had been a paying lodger there and at the time we both had pure white, dyed, spiky hair. One day, the postman came to the door and saw us, and said, 'You two are an odd-looking couple. You're Mr and Mrs Strange,' and it sort of stuck. From then on she was Suzi Strange and I was Steve Strange.

Things were so thrillingly chaotic I didn't even get round to phoning my mum for six months. I didn't mean to worry her, but I was completely obsessed. I felt really guilty when I called her. She had worried so much she had lost three stone in weight. I finally got in touch when I was in the Middlesex Hospital. It was my friend Linda Clarke who realised I was ill. She saw me one day and said, 'What's the matter, Steve? You're yellow.' She called an ambulance and I was rushed to hospital, where I was diagnosed with hepatitis. I'd picked it up after drinking from a cracked cup while I'd been staying at a flat with Glen Matlock's girlfriend Celia, where Sid Vicious also used to turn up looking for a bed. My mum came to visit me, and although she could only see me through a glass partition, it was good to see her again, and I was soon up and about.

Getting ill wasn't unusual. I didn't really have much to do with drugs at the time, except for snorting speed before a gig, but when I went out I would drink heavily. I was having a ball, surviving on virtually nothing, but living the life of Riley.

When I came out of hospital I went to stay with Marco Pirroni, who went on to be in Adam and the Ants. He was still living at home with his mum and dad in Harrow, and they sort of adopted me. They ran a cafe by Warren Street tube station and sometimes I'd work in the cafe to earn some money. My mum went to see Mr and Mrs Pirroni because she was so worried about me, but having met them she was a lot more at ease about me being in London. She could see that they were making sure I was eating better than I had been and she returned to Wales reassured that I was in good hands.

Things were finally starting to fall into place. I had a job. I had a name. I soon had somewhere of my own to live as well – albeit briefly. Someone suggested that Billy Idol – who was also homeless – and I should break into an empty flat in their mansion block and squat there. Billy and I and the Generation X guitarist Derwood moved all of our stuff in, got the electricity going and then had an anarchic decoration idea. We went around the streets nicking old *Evening Standard* billboards that said things like 'Rapist On The Run' and used them to paper the kitchen and hall. The rest of the flat we covered in graffiti. It was great. We had hot water, lighting and we weren't paying any rent. We moved some furniture in and made it a real home from home. It was handy for the West End, and the Moonlight Club, a great small venue for up-and-coming bands, was just around the corner.

We'd been there for about a month when early one morning we heard a noise. Outside, someone with a Middle Eastern accent was shouting, 'You'd better open up.' It sounded very threatening. We were shitting ourselves already, and then we heard the door being smashed in. Through the splinters we could see these huge men carrying sledge-hammers. As they worked their way round the flat we hid in the corner. As soon as we had a chance, we grabbed as much stuff as we could, crammed it into plastic bags, got out down the fire escape and ran for it. Derwood took his life in his hands when he risked sneaking back in for his guitar, but basically we were homeless again and I had to go back to living from sofa to sofa.

By early 1977 the Anarchy Tour was over and punk was becoming more mainstream. I had moved out of the Oval and after a brief spell back on Glen's sofa I moved to Jean-Jacques Burnel's sofa in West Hampstead. I felt like I was closer to the music scene there. Dr Feelgood's guitarist Wilko Johnson and his girlfriend Maria also lived there. Glen had been very helpful. He had introduced me to Malcolm McLaren who had given me some work at his company Glitterbest three days a week, coming up with ideas and poster concepts. I made some good friends, people like Malcolm's secretary Sophie, but they didn't really pay me enough to live on. Luckily Malcolm's partner Vivienne Westwood, who ran Seditionaries, had taken a shine to me, and would give me a discount on her clothes, but the trouble was I never really got the credit for anything I was doing and I was getting increasingly frustrated. One night Billy Idol turned up with some good news. Generation X had now signed a lucrative record contract and he said I could work for them as he had promised.

I was also able to earn decent money working in Seditionaries. Vivienne was always more generous than Malcolm. I earnt more on a Saturday afternoon in her shop than in three days working for Glitterbest. There was a clique of us: Jordan, Debbie, Tracey, Alan Jones and me, and we would go off to gigs together, but after a while the atmosphere changed. I'd go to a Siouxsie and the Banshees gig in a Vivienne Westwood outfit, and the bottom of bill would be a skinhead band or a band like The UK Subs. It got to the stage where in your blood you thought, 'I've got to get out of here or I'm gonna get my head kicked in.' Punk, which was supposed to bring people together, was now dividing them again. An overtone of violence was in the air when these bands were on the bill. All the original rebellious force of punk, and creating your own style, was gone. The *Daily Mirror* was telling you how to rip your clothes and pretend you had a pierced nose. Unbeknown to me at the time, I was getting bored with the scene and I was getting ready to move on.

Through punk's social support system I found somewhere new to live, a squat in the back of beyond, Alperton, near Wembley. It was almost like the punk version of a hippy commune. Jamie Reid, who designed the 'anarchy' poster and the God Save The Queen image with the safety pin in the Queen's lip, was living there with a girl called Barbara. Budgie, who was drumming in The Slits and later ended up in Siouxsie and the Banshees was there. It was a great place, and at last I actually had my own room. Round the corner, my friend Linda Clarke, who went out with a guitarist called John McKay, who played with Siouxsie and the Banshees, had a place. It was quite a little punk village and we all used to make that Monday pilgrimage to the Vortex or to a special gig like The Slits at the Roxy.

One night they did a gig at a comprehensive school in Notting Hill and we all went there; another night an embryonic line-up of Frankie Goes To Hollywood did a gig and stayed at the squat, which was well known in punk circles. The only problem was that it was about ten miles outside central London. Most evenings would end with us doing runners from taxis. We would get the driver to pull up in a nearby street, pretending it was where we lived, and we would jump out of the cab and just run like hell to get away.

We got by on a heady mix of initiative and cheek. We managed to dress well because the guy who started the clothes shop American Retro used to stay in the house and stored his imported clothes there. If we were going out for the night I would rummage in his boxes and pull out jeans, corduroy shirts and baseball jackets. When I got back I'd return them and he never knew they had gone anywhere.

I was always able to overcome the basic problem of not having any money. I used to stand in the street, begging. I must have been one of the first punk panhandlers and I managed to make people take pity on me and dig into their pockets. I'd come back an hour later with £15 in my pocket, ready for a night out.

It was while I was at the Alperton squat that I started to become more ambitious. I was disillusioned by punk and felt it would be nice to be in a band or even kick-start something myself. I had already met some of the colourful characters that felt the same way. I was walking across Piccadilly Circus one day when I heard a camp voice shout out, 'Look at her in her Vivienne Westwood suit. Where are you going?' It was Philip Sallon, who had been a bit of a face on the London scene for years. He was with Boy George, then just plain George O'Dowd. Philip said they were going off to the Global Village and he invited me along. That was how we got to know each other. After a while, and a few drinks, George and I got talking and we both agreed that we were bored with punk and wished something else would happen.

I was always on the lookout for better work and a better place to stay, and by chance the two came about at the same time. Things weren't really working out with Generation X, and Glen's post-Pistols band, The Rich Kids, was one of the bright hopes on EMI. The band had an office in Marylebone High Street, right in the centre of London. I offered to help out with the running of the fan club and coming up with ideas for the group's outfits, which Celia, Glen's then-girlfriend, would design. This meant that I had to have keys to the office, which was pretty handy when it came to dossing somewhere in town late at night . . .

I was getting a bit of a name on the punk scene and I got talking to some of the others in the house about forming a band. Dave Goodman, a producer who fancied himself as a bit of a McLaren-type figure, had an idea for a band. He suggested to me and Chrissie Hynde, who was also part of punk's inner circle and was desperate to be in a band, that we put these paper bags on our heads and call ourselves The Moors Murderers. Now, I was too young to know about the Moors Murderers, and Chrissie, being American, didn't have a clue, but we went ahead with the photo shoot. At the press call we put hoods over our heads and announced that our début single on the Popcorn label would be called Free Myra Hindley, backed by a new version of The 10 Commandments. My stage name was Steve Brady and Chrissie's name was Christine Hindley. Some of the lyrics to Free Myra Hindley were as follows:

> In nineteen hundred and sixty four
> Myra Hindley was nothing more than a woman who fell for a man.
>> So why can't she be free?
>> Free Hindley!
>
> Brady was her lover, he told her what to do
>> A psychopathic killer, nothing new
>> So why can't she be free?
>> Free Hindley!

Stories immediately appeared in the *Sunday Mirror*, the *News of the World* and the *People* condemning us as the sickest punk band yet. Dave Goodman had gone for pure shock tactics to promote the non-existent single.

That was my first real experience of the press and it frightened the shit out of me. It made me well known but not in the way I had intended. People wanted to kill me. Even punks wanted to kill me. I said to Chrissie, 'I don't want anything to do with this charade.' We hadn't even recorded anything yet, never mind released it, as the papers had made out. It was hard enough getting a band together.

Chrissie and I had just done a bit of rehearsing, and we decided to try writing together. Basically we just came up with songs about criminals – something about the Krays and one half-decent song about gangsters, called Chicago: Caesar of Crime – 'A rose in his buttonhole, a diamond solitaire, loud-mouthed public enemy number one, the man behind Thompson's submachine gun.' We put an ad in *Melody Maker* to form a band, but Chrissie was a hard taskmaster. If the drummer couldn't keep up, he was out, and eventually we ran out of drummers.

One of the people who had seen us rehearsing was Andrew Czezowski and his lovely wife Sue. He ran the Roxy, but he was about to leave there and wanted to put his mark on something new. He seemed to like my style and, realising I had a talent for making a bit of a name for myself, he asked me if I would front a band he was putting together called The Photons. Czezowski thought that punk was nearing its end and he wanted to be first in with the next big thing, which had been dubbed powerpop. The timing was good for me because I'd broken ties with Vivienne and Malcolm, and hooked up with another couple in the fashion trade called Helen and Steph Robinson. They had originally had half a share in Boy, which was the rival to Vivienne's original punk shop, Sex. They had then split from Boy and started up PX, getting me in to run the shop because I was a face on the scene. I already had a following of kids who copied whatever I was wearing and Andrew wanted The Photons to wear special outfits that he had designed, in the same way that The Sex Pistols wore Malcolm and Vivienne's clothes. The links between the band and the shop were already there. The Photons even rehearsed in rooms under PX in Covent Garden, at the time when it was still a fruit market.

We quickly set up a mini-tour of about eight gigs, ending with a big showcase in Covent Garden. It was fun to do and a great learning experience, but I realised very quickly that the band wasn't going anywhere for two reasons: firstly I didn't get on with the drummer and secondly the clothes felt too much like uniforms. 'Photons' means particles of light, and the idea was that we all wore different coloured suits, bright reds and yellows with big, billowing sleeves in complete contrast to the dowdy blacks and greys of punk. But when it got to the

London gig we had three days off and I knew that everyone from the punk scene would be there: Mick Jones and Joe Strummer from The Clash, Billy Idol, Don Letts, Siouxsie, Sid Vicious and Glen Matlock, Midge Ure and Rusty Egan from The Rich Kids. I went to a designer friend of mine and asked for something special to be made for the gig, so that I didn't look like part of the regiment. The band didn't know I'd done this. They went on stage, and I said, 'I'll be there in a minute.' I quickly ran into the toilet and got out of my red suit. When I came out, their jaws dropped and they said, 'What the fuck has Steve got on?' I didn't do it to cause an argument in the band, but deep down I think I knew this London show might be the last gig. I thought I might go on to have a solo career; I didn't know how things would work out. I didn't plan to start a nightlife revolution.

Despite the band's shock, the gig went down fairly well. Afterwards, Midge Ure came backstage. Things weren't working out with The Rich Kids. Midge and Glen were pulling in different musical directions and neither were getting much support from the record company. Midge was getting more into electronic music, Glen was a rock and roller at heart. It looked like they wouldn't record again. Midge liked my approach and said, 'Look, I've got some Rich Kids studio time owing to me from EMI. I've got an idea for a new project. It won't cost anything. Let's see what comes together.' And that's how I got involved in Visage.

I knew how songs were put together after rehearsing with Chrissie and then The Photons. I didn't go to Midge blind. This was also my way of getting out of The Photons. The project seemed perfect and there was quite a bit of interest in the demos when we started to circulate them. We did cover versions of two classic songs from the sixties, the doomy In the Year 2525 by Zager and Evans, and the apocalyptic warning Eve of Destruction, by Barry McGuire. We also tried out our own composition, All The King's Horses. The main thing Midge and I agreed on was that we shouldn't sign to EMI. They had not promoted The Rich Kids very well at all, virtually writing them off as a tax loss when the first single wasn't an immediate hit. I suppose I was very ambitious, although I didn't see myself like that. Later on everyone would say to me, 'You had so much ambition.' What I did know was that whatever I set out to do, I would make it work, whether it was music or fashion.

Rusty Egan also worked on the demos and I got to know him much better. Rusty is one of London's great characters, a copper-haired kid, a non-stop talker, who in his time had been a record company messenger boy and aspiring drummer. His parents had run an Irish showband, the Bernie Egan combo, which was where he learnt to play. His upfront confidence had once earnt him an audition with The Clash, but he hadn't quite made it into the band. In the end he had landed the gig with The Rich Kids. I remember my first meeting with Rusty at a Jam gig at the Red Cow pub in Hammersmith around Spring 1977. He was so loud I could hear him talking about me from across the bar, 'It's that guy again 'oo always looks great. 'e looks like 'e should be in a band. 'oo is 'e?' The next thing I knew he was behind me, trying to nick my leather Gestapo coat. I'd keep bumping into him because it was such a close-knit scene. He now claims that I used to work at the Roxy, cleaning the toilets, but I didn't.

I'd see Rusty at the Hope and Anchor in Islington, the Vortex off Oxford Street and the Roxy in Covent Garden. To be honest, whenever I saw him I would cringe because he would shout things about me across crowded pubs such as, 'Don't that geezer look amazing, 'e's got such a great look.' I would hide my head when I saw him walking down the King's Road, but he always seemed to spot me first.

We had a bit of a love–hate relationship, but Rusty became my saviour. He had heard about me sleeping in The Rich Kids' office, and knew I wanted to live somewhere more central. One day he said, 'Look, I'm living in Harley Street Mews West. It's nothing flash, but you are welcome to sleep on the sofa.' I was signing on and getting very little money, so I jumped at the chance to move in with Rusty and a female friend of his. He always seemed to have a girl on the go. The move finally cemented our friendship. We ended up working together for eight years, and are still friends now, but sometimes I wonder how. He's the kind of friend who never stops talking for long enough to listen to what you have to say. He might pause for a moment, but then he will just carry on as if he hasn't heard a word you've said. He can be his own worst enemy. Some people thought we were lovers, particularly when we lived together, but there has definitely never been anything sexual between Rusty and me.

By the time I did the demo with Midge and Rusty I was very disillusioned with the punk thing. Rusty felt the same way too, and we decided maybe others were looking for something different as well. I had been over to France when The Sex Pistols had done a gig there, and I'd heard a lot of European music. By coincidence, Rusty had spent some time in Berlin, where he had discovered electronic bands such as Kraftwerk and Nina Hagen.

One day, Rusty and I were chatting about how things had gone a bit stagnant. We were talking about London clubs and comparing them to those in other cities. The only one that was anything like New York's Studio 54, running different clubs for different scenes on different nights, was the Embassy Club, which catered for a classier, older clientele. We thought that we could do the same thing for a younger, hipper set. We were young and had the balls to do anything, so we looked for a venue where we could set up our own club. We were very shrewd. We went to Billy's, a club at 69 Dean Street, on a Tuesday, and saw that it was empty. It was a venue with a great past. When it had been known as the Gargoyle club before the war, both Noel Coward and Tallulah Bankhead were members. But it had clearly seen better days. The people hanging out there were mostly Soho's sex workers, grabbing a breather.

Two weeks later we went back to the owner and said we could pack the club. He could have the drinks' profits and we would take the money on the door. It didn't occur to us for a moment that no one would turn up. We printed up flyers with the tantalising line, 'Fame Fame Jump Aboard the Night Train/Fame, Fame, Fame. What's Your Name?' We opened in Autumn 1978 and very quickly we were successful. All the punks who were also closet David Bowie fans turned up. Soon it was a regular event known as Bowie Night. In the end though, it became ridiculous. Even though it was still an underground, word-of-mouth scene, more people were being turned away than we could fit into the club, which had a capacity of 250. Queues were stretching round the block. This was without any support from the press. There weren't any live bands so the *New Musical Express* and other inky music papers weren't interested, and the *Face* and *i-D* hadn't been founded yet. We had tapped into something bigger than we had imagined.

There was clearly a like-minded crowd for what we were doing. There were people who had created unique identities for themselves, like Philip Sallon. Boy George was there in his kimono, Stephen Linard in his tartan Culloden outfit, Marilyn, Claire the Hair and Tranny Paul. Pinkietessa, formerly known as Theresa Thurmer, was a secretary at the *Daily Express* by day, but by night she changed her name and dressed like an all-pink, home-made version of Bo Peep. The milliner Stephen Jones was there. So was the designer Kim Bowen, and Melissa Caplan, Simon Withers and Lee Sheldrick. Influential stylists Michael Kostiff and his wife Gelinda, who has since sadly died, would pop in. The film-maker John Maybury, who at the time was the boyfriend of the artist Kevin Whitney, was a regular. Everyone made an effort to look as different as possible, drawing inspiration for their looks from the unlikeliest of places. One night David Claridge and Daniel James turned up as characters from Thunderbirds. St Martin's was at its height of creativity, and the bright sparks of the fashion department seemed to be using the club as its common room. People stood in the Soho rain in gold braid and pill box hats, waiting to get in. Cossacks and queens mingled happily as narcissism ran riot. Billy's attracted a clique of outrageous people like a magnet. It was bizarre. All these people were dressed like royalty, while in reality they were just ex-punks running up the clothes on their mum's sewing machines at home in the suburbs or living in the nearby squats in Warren Street and Great Titchfield Street. At Billy's we were all clocking each other to see who was more outrageous. The people who turned up were a bit of a mish-mash, but what they all had in common was that they were fed up with punk, and had a love of David Bowie. Rusty, who DJ'd, tried not to play much punk music, so there was a lot of Bowie on the turntables, along with futuristic German music, Being Boiled by The Human League, Warm Leatherette by The Normal, the theme from Stingray and torch songs from Marlene Dietrich. Rusty didn't think of himself as a DJ though. He was just the bloke who put the records on. As there wasn't much music to play he also played the electronic demos we had done with Midge Ure, which went down very well. In the Year 2525 and Eve of Destruction were old songs, but they seemed to fit in with the mood of a gathering that was signalling the end of one era and the beginning of another. It was decadent, and evocative of Berlin cabaret in the thirties.

Because the club was so busy, I stood at the entrance in my leather jodhpurs and German overcoat, deciding who could come in. I was strict on the door because once people were inside I didn't want them to feel they were in a goldfish bowl. I wanted them to feel they were in their own place amongst friends, and that anything went. Just because guys were wearing more make-up and there were gay overtones, it didn't mean a guy was gay. Once inside the small, sweaty downstairs room, customers were greeted by an unusual atmosphere. The club was in the heart of Soho, and was still frequented by pimps and hookers. The hookers didn't create bad vibes, but the pimps occasionally made people feel uncomfortable, because some of our crowd were scantily dressed and the pimps were intimidating. But, apart from that, everyone mixed freely, there was rarely any hassle. The only real problem came from the owner. We had kept our promise of filling his club up, but after three months we realised it was time to move on because we needed bigger premises. Once the owner heard we were thinking of leaving, he threatened Rusty, because he wanted to keep the winning formula. Rusty got paranoid and went into hiding, but we had no choice but to make the move to somewhere bigger. The nightclub revolution had begun.

CHAPTER FOUR

THE CULT WITH NO NAME

On 6 February 1979 Bowie Night moved to a much bigger club on the other side of Covent Garden. Blitz was a wine bar on Great Queen Street, near Holborn tube station, decorated with images of World War Two, such as murals of St Paul's Cathedral under fire and warplanes flying overhead. The Bowie Night name was soon dropped as the club developed a unique identity of its own. Every Tuesday, 350 of the most creative, individualistic young people in London would cram into the club. Many were ex-punks, fed up with a scene that had burnt brightly, but all too quickly turned in on itself. Others were young fashion students from the nearby St Martin's College on Charing Cross Road turning the place into a personal catwalk.

Queues were soon forming around the block again, and I was busy all night on the door. There were no bouncers back then, and no clipboard and guest list printed up in advance – just me. I was very strict about everyone paying. I'd say, 'This is not a charity, at the end of the day this is our job and we are working hard at it.' It was not hard to decide who to let in and who to leave out. People thought they could get in just by looking ridiculous, but that was not the point. I wanted people to be stylish. There was one man who turned up one night in a rubber wet suit. I told him to get back to the river. If someone turned up and had just painted their face half black and half white, I would knock them back because it simply wasn't right. Maybe people thought we looked like prats, but a lot of thought went into the way we put our clothes together. It was about finding your own creativity inside yourself.

I made a lot of enemies by trying to make the club look good. Barely a night would go by when I wasn't spat at at least once. An evening would not be complete without someone threatening to punch me out. But, despite appearances, I could handle myself physically. I'd grown up in south Wales, where you had to be tough to survive. Those playground punch-ups stood me in good stead.

Maybe a lot of it was escapism, but for me, it wasn't just dressing up for the night. By day, I was now working in PX, and these were my work clothes. We all loved the attention. Kim Bowen used to work behind the checkout desk at the Virgin Megastore in Oxford Street while she was living at the Warren Street squat. One day she turned up for work dressed as Queen Elizabeth I, in full, flowing robes. She strutted round the shop and enjoyed the looks she was getting so much that she continued to walk up and down Tottenham Court Road just for the fun of it.

People involved in the art and fashion world were instinctively drawn to Blitz. Zandra Rhodes came down and invited me over to her house for dinner because she thought I looked interesting. Andrew Logan and Duggie Fields, the freaks of their generation, came down to check out the new talent. Designer Nicky Haslam was always dropping in. All the young fashion names were there, following me from Billy's and telling their friends about the club: Melissa Caplan, Stephen Linnard, Kim Bowen, Michelle Clapton, John Galliano and Julia Fodor. There were all sorts of misfits and oddballs such as Barry the Rat, who always took his rat clubbing. Nobody had any money, a lot of them were living in the squats around Warren Street with the designers and the likes of George O'Dowd and Marilyn, but they all knew how to look good on a pittance. They would turn up dressed to the nines and there was fierce competition to see which one could get the biggest picture in the papers.

The club was a platform for new talent. Apart from the fashion crowd, there was journalist Robert Elms, who wrote about the scene, and photographers Gabor Scott and David Johnson who recorded the visuals for posterity. Ben Kelly, who went on to design the Hacienda in Manchester, was part of the crowd. So was David Claridge, the man who invented Roland Rat. Until we came along, London clubland had been in the doldrums. It hadn't swung since the sixties. Together we gave nightlife a kick up the backside in the same way that punk rock gave a kick up the backside to the music industry.

The brilliant thing was that everyone involved had a role. George was in the cloakroom in his white-faced kabuki make-up and kimono, Rusty, in his fifties suits, played the records, and I was on the door in my high hair and high heels, carrying a silver-topped cane. I only ever tried DJing once, on a night when I tried to set up a kind of cafe society, playing Shirley Bassey, Dusty Springfield, Frank Sinatra and escalator background music. But I only dabbled, because I was always needed on the door. Until I met Blitz regular Rosemary Turner, I didn't trust anyone else to do the door. She watched me to learn my techniques and then she was ready to do it herself. My door policy was always very strict. Membership was £2, entry was £1 and everyone had to pay – even the regular faces and the people who would become Spandau Ballet. If people didn't want to pay, and thought they were above it, I'd say, 'Who the fuck are you?'

Of course, the same things went on in our clubs that had always gone on in clubs. Sex was rampant, and everybody seemed to know everybody. If somebody copped off with a girl and didn't have anywhere to go, they always knew that Warren Street was available, because it was the squat where anything went.

Look back at the pictures of Blitz or the documentaries and you'd think it was a poseurs' paradise, the home of the beautiful people, but it wasn't always like that. People were often either speeding or drunk. There was plenty of glamour, but it was also very debauched. There was always someone falling over. The men were always in the ladies' loos putting their make-up on because it had the best mirrors. Sometimes you'd walk into the loos and the scent of hairspray would almost knock you out. But one thing you can say about Blitz is that there were no barriers. The women didn't feel threatened at all by men using their toilets.

Gradually the media started to pick up on the success of Blitz. Boy George was becoming known in his own right, but I was the one who was initially singled out and courted by the press because of my striking appearance, and because I was the one with the power to allow people in. I'd be invited to glitzy showbiz parties and everything was wonderful. There was free drink and free food. As soon as I arrived at a gallery opening or a launch party, I'd just down as much champagne as I could get my hands on and fill my empty stomach with the food that was available.

With a bit of money in my pocket, at last I started to live better. I started to frequent the Speakeasy in Soho, where rock stars would hang out on their days off. Pete Townshend was a regular there and The Sex Pistols had once been involved in a fracas there when they confronted Bob Harris and asked him why he never played their records.

Going out in London was much more fun with a bit of cash in your pocket. It was the era of cocktails and decadence, Long Island Teas and Banana Dacquiries. Every now and again I'd meet up with Billy Idol and we would go to Trader Vic's cocktail bar under the Hilton. I'd get completely bombed there. We just used to order a big cocktail in a bowl with a straw each, and by the time you'd had a couple of those you wouldn't even remember where you were.

There was drinking all the time. We never needed much of an excuse for a party. It was ironic that England was about to sink into an economic recession, but then they say you party the hardest when the ship is sinking. Failure could not have been further from our minds. We seemed to be having a great time. Business was booming.

Everything was going well at Blitz. George and I were being seen at parties, and a day later it would be in a gossip column as the national newspapers tried to give a name to the movement. The *Face* and *i-D* had started and they were reporting on the scene as well, dubbing it the Cult With No Name, the Blitz Kids and the Now Crowd. Pick up the *Evening Standard,* and there was my stark, white face, scarlet lipstick, jet black, spiky hair 12 inches high, steamed and crimped with steel steamers, staring out at you. We didn't get any coverage in the *New Musical Express* or *Melody Maker* because that sort of paper liked to think that they had discovered you, make you their darlings, build you up, and then knock you down. We didn't care, we were making it without their support, having gone straight into the mainstream. Life felt good. We weren't making a fortune at Blitz but we were starting to live well after years on the breadline. Rusty and I were taking a wage of about £150 a week – quite a lot back then – and we decided to move into a better flat. We found a place in Clanricarde Gardens in Notting Hill where Karen O'Connor, the light entertainer Des O'Connor's daughter, lived with another friend, Buki. I knew Karen because she used to go out with Billy Idol. Rusty and I had single beds in the same room, Karen had a room and Buki had a room. There was also a living room, but by now no one ever seemed to use it. We were always out partying or working. Usually both.

One night the film-maker Lyndall Hobbs came down to Blitz to do a documentary on us called Stepping Out in London, which went out as a support feature to the first Alien movie – appropriate really, as a lot of people thought we looked like aliens. The crowd that night was a slightly special one, because it had a theme of Come as Your Favourite Blonde. Marilyn was very clever. He used to be just plain Peter Robinson from Borehamwood, but by the time he had moved to Warren Street he would wear some sort of support to make him look like he had a cleavage. He was the spitting image of Marilyn Monroe, which was perfect the night the cameras were in. Marilyn became a real prima donna when he had a hit single, but he was fairly bad back then too, wanting to look just right for the cameras. And you had to watch your things when Marilyn was about. Nothing serious, but if you turned your back your can of hairspray would be gone. Others came as Jayne Mansfield or just painted their faces white. I was the Milky Bar Kid.

Casting directors were always coming down to Blitz looking for people to add a bit of colour and exoticism to their movies. I was asked to be in a crowd scene in the hit movie Breaking Glass. A lot of the Blitz crowd was used as extras but I was treated a bit better than most. People like Boy George had to hang around all day, but after I had done my bit I was given an envelope with my money in it and I was able to go home.

I always had an on–off friendship with George. He says that I gave him the cloakroom job to make him feel small and then I sacked him for nicking money from people's pockets. There was no way that when Blitz took off I gave him a job in the cloakroom to belittle him. I knew the people who lived in the Warren Street squat were desperate for money and if I could help them out I would give them a job. I'd just got lucky and I was trying to be kind, but he took it the wrong way.

The success of the club had its downside too. There were so many people turning up that I was getting into trouble with the owners for letting too many people in. We'd frequently get visits from the fire brigade warning us about breaching safety regulations. Eventually I was warned that if we were caught over capacity again the club would lose its licence. I didn't want that to happen. Everyone, not only me, would have been out of a job.

It was just my luck that soon after this confrontation, a quite drunk Mick Jagger turned up at the door with his entourage. It has always been said that I held a mirror up to his wrinkly face, as I did with a lot of potential customers, and said, 'Would you let yourself in?' Although I did pick on people who didn't have the right look, sadly that's not what happened at all. I explained what had happened with the fire officer to Mick's friends, who were more sober. Meanwhile Mick was getting annoyed, saying, 'Don't you know who I am?' I tried to be polite and his friends tried to calm him down as he went off in search of nightlife elsewhere. But it just happened that a tabloid journalist was there at the time. By the following day, the story had got out, with typical press embellishment, and the legend of Blitz being the ultra-exclusive club for the new young élite was established.

After that coverage things just escalated. The tabloids became obsessed with what we were wearing every week. It was about a month later, in July, when we had a visit from my childhood idol, David Bowie. There had already been rumours that his Boys Keep Swinging video, in which he donned lip gloss and dressed up as various women, had been inspired by some of the sartorial antics at Billy's, and Bowie was always keen to throw himself into the latest, coolest trends, so it should not really have been a surprise when he appeared unannounced. But despite my outward show of calm, inside I had butterflies, wondering what he wanted and what he would think of Blitz. We had no prior warning, and he arrived with two other people and his PA Coco, whom I didn't think was very nice. We managed to sneak them into the club the back way to avoid a fuss and usher him upstairs to a private area. David himself was charming and asked if I would join him upstairs for a drink when I had finished on the door. I wanted to go straight away but, annoyingly, I had to do my job first and stay at the door.

Word soon spread like wildfire that David Bowie was there. He was probably the reason most people at the club had got into pop music in the first place. Travel back to the childhood bedroom of most Blitz *habitués* and you'd find a David Bowie poster on the wall. He had changed his look and his sound so many times, there were more than enough images to go round. The alien from Low and The Man Who Fell To Earth. Aladdin Sane. Diamond Dogs. Ziggy Stardust. He was the one person that everyone there would cite as an influence, even more important than punk. Everyone wanted to go upstairs and see him. We had to have extra security to keep people back. He said it was a great scene and asked me if I would like to appear in the video for his next single, Ashes to Ashes. He also asked me if I could suggest a make-up artiste for him, and I recommended Richard Sharah, the man who did my make-up. Imagine, when I was a 13-year-old boy, this man had been my ultimate hero. I just couldn't believe it. He then said to me, 'Look, I'd like it left to you to pick the clothes you are going to wear, and to choose three other extras for the video. But there is only one snag. We have to meet tomorrow morning at 6am outside the Hilton to leave for the location shoot.' Blitz didn't finish until 2.30am and I didn't usually get home until 3.30am. This was the most important moment of my life. I rushed around and found Judith Franklin, Darla Jane Gilroy and another girl for the video, and told them they had to be ready and at the Hilton by 6am.

As soon as the club closed I rushed home and sorted out my outfit. We had quickly agreed that we should all dress as gothic, ecclesiastical priests, in black and white, topped off with beads and crucifixes. The Vatican always was a great source of inspiration. I had a long gown on and a kind of netted beekeeper's hat designed by Stephen Jones, and was all ready to be jetted off to a glamorous location. Barbados? Spain? Paris? The coach arrived, and we were told where we were going. Southend.

As it turned out, a kiss-me-quick hat was not required. It may have sounded tacky and not at all what I expected from David Bowie, but I have really fond memories of the video shoot, my first of many. It was done on a quiet beach which had been closed off to the public. It seemed like a very long day for a three-minute film. The basic plot for the day involved David Bowie in a pierrot outfit, much like the one I had been wearing at Blitz, walking along the beach followed by me and the girls and then a bulldozer. Don't ask me what it was meant to mean, though I'm sure David and the director David Mallett were striving for something in particular . . .

The difficulty was getting us all to move along at the correct speed. If I was too fast, I caught David up; if I was too slow, the bulldozer kept catching the robe I was wearing. There's a famous moment in it where it looks as if I am bending forward to bow. What I was actually doing was moving the hem of my robe to avoid getting pulled over by the bulldozer, but they decided to keep it in. It was a real learning experience about the length of time a video takes, but throughout the day I could not stop thinking that I was actually working with the man I had worshipped as a teenager. I had queued outside a record shop in Pontypool to buy his new album when I was 13, and now he wanted to work with me. When I was handing out flyers for Billy's I'd never thought something like this would happen, but the clubs were beginning to pay off. This certainly felt like the beginning of the fulfilment of a dream. I was delighted when I was handed my wages of £50 by a grateful member of the production team. It had been hard, nerve-wracking, demanding work, but worth every second. And I was determined that this would not be my last time in front of the cameras. I didn't tell them, but I would have paid them to have appeared in a video with David Bowie.

By the end of the day I was still completely in awe of Bowie. On the coach coming back to London everyone was exhausted but animated.

This was our first brush with real stardom. But I also had something else on my mind. I had been so wrapped up in the filming that I realised that I had not even been to the toilet. I was so desperate for the bog that I pissed into an empty beer bottle which I held under my ecclesiastical robes. The trouble was I had drunk so much water while I had been standing around waiting for the cameras to roll that I couldn't stop peeing, and the bottle overflowed. There was piss trailing all the way along the coach from the back to the front.

As well as Blitz, I was also still working with PX, the clothes shop in Covent Garden. In many respects PX, formed by Helen and Steph Robinson, became the house designer for the New Romantic scene, as it was now called. Having cut their teeth selling their designs from a market stall, Helen and Steph opened the first PX shop in James Street off Covent Garden in September 1978, using old disused fittings from MI5's Curzon Street offices, which had recently closed down. By the time we opened at Billy's they had a good line in German military gear, making their own idiosyncratic versions complete with diamante when they couldn't get hold of the originals. When we started Blitz I wore their frilly velvet suits with a stark white puritan collar, despite the fact that most of these were sold to women.

I continued to wear the latest looks from PX as they thrived and moved to better premises in nearby Endell Street. I was like a walking advert for them. If I wore something one night, the run would be sold out by the following lunchtime. They did my Robin Hood jackets and pigskin trousers that were laced up the sides. I got the matching hat with the two-foot feather to go with it from Stephen Jones who set up his business in their basement. It was a hugely influential shop. It was doing frilly white blouse-shirts long before Princess Di started to set a trend for them and the high street stores followed. If only I'd had shares in PX I would have made a fortune. But money was the last thing on my mind at the time, as long as I had enough for a drink. I didn't really care about money. The more I had, the more I would have squandered.

As the focal point of the whole scene it was particularly important

My lovely mum forever. Gill Harrington, Carnival Queen.

above Looking smart and showing an early sense of style with my (younger!) Uncle Wayne.

left Aged ten and making sure my precious sister Tanya doesn't come to any harm.

Hey punks, meet t

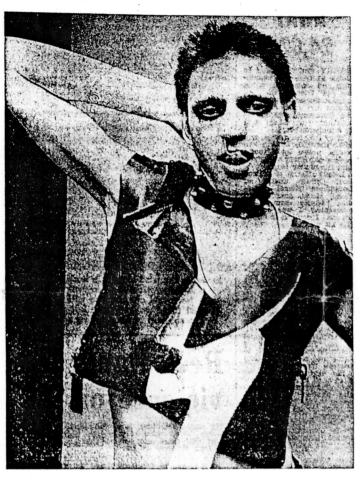

● Punk rock cult boy Colin Fisher with eye make-up, studded collar and a chain hanging from his nose.

As long as the neighbours don't see them dressed up like that

PUNK ROCK, the latest teen cult, has arrived in South Wa

Followers of the new cr wear chains through rings in th noses and ears and dangle ra blades from safety pins in their lobes.

Some of the punk rock boys dress in tights and wear make The girls and boys, both with sh cropped hair, emerged this wee the Stowaway Club in Newport.

They were there to see p rock's heroes—a group called Pistol. The group have a reputat of being unpredictable and spec ise in insulting the audience. T act has been banned in seve parts of London after viol scenes.

Cardiff promoter Andy Wa said many promoters refused handle them because of their un dictable performances. Punk re he said, was music with vio visuals. The group also shou obsenities at the audience.

The manager of the Stowa Club, Mr. Martin Noone, although there was no trouble would definitely not be having group back. "I didn't believe eyes when I saw the youngs coming in," he said.

"I had a very uneasy evenin saw one boy pull a length of v from his sleeve and hold it betw his hands as if he was going garrotte someone."

Devotee Mark Taylor, aged

above *Western Mail*, September 1976. Making my media debut as the firs punk in Wales, causing outrage following a riotous Sex Pistols gig in Newport.

left New romantic aristocrats. With Monty (left) and Chessie (right) on *Top Of The Pops*. Suit by Antony Price.

chain gang

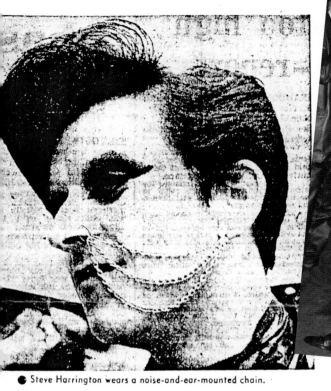

● Steve Harrington wears a noise-and-ear-mounted chain.

chdy Road, Gabalfa, Cardiff,
ack tights, earrings in his
d a silver collar. He said the
ockers "don't bother with
just booze and music."

st of us are punk rock
s. My mother does not mind
I dress but the boys down
ks where I work think I'm
e just do what we want to,
older generation used to be
Boys.

e don't like violence but are

always ready to meet it when it
comes," said Mark, who was wearing make-up and plastic shoes.

Steve Harrington, aged 17, of
Pen-y-Caeau Court, Pantside, Newbridge, was wearing a black plastic
jumpsuit with three chains suspended from rings in his nose and left
ear.

"It's just the fashion. All my
parents worry about is the neighbours," said Steve, who is unem-
ployed.

above right Hanging out
at Billy's in Soho with a
drink, a cigarette and club
regular, Andy.

right Nice clothes,
shame about the carpet.
Relaxing at Billy's,
cossack-style, with
girl-about-town
Jeanette Lee.

Leaders of the new romantic pack. Visage takes shape. From left to right Midge Ure, Rusty Egan, me, Dave Formula and Billy Currie.

THE DAMNED DON'T CRY
VISAGE

left The defining look of the cult with no name: cockatoo hair and Little Lord Fauntleroy collar.

above right Spandau Ballet were taking off but Martin and Gary always had time for a night out at The Camden Palace

below right With Kim Wilde. Rumours of our romance were greatly exaggerated by the press, but the publicity didn't do either of our careers any harm

On tour with the Visage supervixens, Perri Lister (middle) and Lorraine Whitmarsh (right)

Ron Wood and his future wife Jo with Jenny Belle Star unwinding at The Camden Palace after dinner at Langans.

Cigarettes and alcohol with Britt Ekland and her beau, Stray Cat Slim Jim.

St Valentine's Day Massacre Ball at the Camden Palace with Chessie, the sweetest moll in town.

for me to stay one step ahead, so I was constantly looking through history books, old film magazines and design articles, trying to come up with ideas for new images. I almost forgot what my natural hair colour was. I'd model myself on Bonnie Prince Charlie, complete with tartan. Or I'd do something with a hint of the French Revolution about it, with black tousled hair, red lips and heavy mascara. Make-up helped me to change dramatically. I dyed my hair blonde, tanned my face with the aid of a bottle, nurtured a bit of stubble long before George Michael, put on a billowing yellow blouse, brown leather breeches and waistcoat, and came up with a striking Robinson Crusoe image which was featured in a *Sunday Times* fashion spread. I walked with a cane. I went for a swashbuckling look. Anything to be different. Anything to stay ahead of the pack.

When I wasn't wearing clothes from PX there was another great place to get something cheap and unique. It just so happened that around this time there was a massive three-storey costumers' warehouse in Covent Garden, called Charles Fox, being auctioned off. Everything was for sale. It was like being let loose in a fancy dress shop. There were full-length, fox fur coats for £2.50. Arabian prince's costumes with baggy trousers that tucked into black jackboots for a fiver. Because the clothes were intended for theatrical use, everything had a very over-the-top style. I was particularly fond of a cape, with matching gold embroidery, that went over one shoulder.

Charles Fox was also a good place to pick up exotic make-up. Over the years my make-up technique had improved dramatically. I was wearing make-up when I went out in Newport and Cardiff, but it was very basic. By now though I was starting to do photo shoots and I started to pick up tricks from make-up artistes such as Richard Sharah, who used to help me out. As time progressed I became more and more creative. I saw how a look could be changed dramatically with a different type of make-up. Charles Fox had various weird and wonderful colours of foundation for productions that might have needed to turn humans into animals, and they were selling it off at ridiculous prices. I think the odd eye-liner fell into my pocket too. Back at the flat, where others might have kept a toolkit full of screwdrivers and spanners, I filled my toolkit with make-up. It was a healthy creative scene. Designers sold their clothes to other punters and part-time models, and their careers started to blossom as their designs appeared in Sunday supplement fashion spreads.

As Blitz started to take off, bands started to form, inspired by the scene, and copycat clubs started to open around the country. Basildon's very own Essex futurists Depeche Mode cut their teeth at Crocs in Rayleigh and popped down to Blitz to pick up some tips. Duran Duran became the house band at Birmingham's Rum Runner club. At Blitz itself, there was a group of experimental dancers known as Shock, and Kenny Everett's dancers, Hot Gossip, used to perform a much ruder act than they were ever allowed to do on television. But most famously Spandau Ballet emerged from Blitz. Gary Kemp, Martin Kemp, Steve Norman, John Keeble, Tony Hadley and their manager Steve Dagger were ambitious, working-class Islington lads who had gone through the same process as me – from soul boy to punk – and were now looking for some new youth culture they could call their own. They had been a band for a while, but Blitz gave them an identity and a style, and Robert Elms gave them a name, having seen it written as graffiti on a trip to Germany. Spandau Ballet played one of their earliest shows at the club in December 1979. On 24 January 1980 they played only their fourth gig as Spandau Ballet at Blitz. They had a huge buzz about them. Other bands, including members of The Banshees, The Skids, Ultravox, Magazine, Thin Lizzy and Japan, came along to see what all the fuss was about. By now, record companies were waving cheque books at them. They had an instant audience – the people who had been standing next to them at the bar at Blitz the previous week. Chris Blackwell, the head of Island Records, started talking to their manager, Steve Dagger, when the band had barely started to perform. Blackwell failed to sign them and went on to nurture the synthesiser phase of Grace Jones's career. Some say he was inspired by that night of electronic music at Blitz.

Martin Kemp and I became good friends because his first serious girlfriend was my old punk friend Wendy, who would travel down to Blitz from Borehamwood every Tuesday. Sometimes I'd go up there to visit her. When I got off the train in Borehamwood in my make-up and ecclesiastical robes I would get horrified looks, but that was all part of the fun.

I always fancied Martin and I also thought Steve Norman was very sexy. We used to laugh about it because they were definitely straight and we all knew nothing sexual was ever going to happen between us. There was one drunken occasion when Steve and Martin both woke up in my bed, but it was all purely innocent.

We always had a good laugh together. There was a time when I was in New York with Steve, and I picked up a copy of the *Fetish Times*. We couldn't believe some of the contact ads in the magazine. I'm pretty broadminded, but even I was shocked. It became a bit of an in-joke between the three of us that I'd always try to chat them up and get them 'back to my house for coffee'. One night, just Steve stayed over at my house. I said to him recently, 'Do you remember that night we had wild, passionate sex?' He laughed, and replied, 'There might have been wild passionate sex for you but there was none for me.'

One night I was at the Embassy club in Bond Street with Boy George when we were approached by Elton John. He had taken a shine to me and invited us to his gig at the Hammersmith Odeon. Elton's manager John Reid telephoned me the next day and said that he would lay everything on for us, and what time would we like to be picked up. On the night, a Rolls Royce pulled up outside my house at 7.30pm on the dot. George and I were like two excited school kids. We didn't want to go straight to the gig, we wanted to stop off everywhere to show off. When we got there, we were treated like royalty. We were taken down to Elton's dressing room where the champagne flowed. Afterwards the Rolls Royce took us home, and once again we stopped off wherever we could, with the windows down to make sure everyone had seen us.

There was never enough time in the day to do everything. The burgeoning club was taking up more and more of my time. From Blitz we expanded and opened another Covent Garden club, Hell, at 30 Henrietta Street, which was pretty much in the same vein as Blitz, but this time Rusty and I were helped by Chris Sullivan, my old mate from Merthyr Tydfil, who had moved up to London. The look there was in keeping with the name, darker and gloomier, with a bigger emphasis on ecclesiastical garb. As Blitz went overground, Hell stayed underground. In fact, the private party that kicked it off was literally underground.

The opening of Hell coincided with my 21st birthday, so I was determined to come up with something special. In those days, the Circle Line on the London Underground had pubs on various platforms: Sloane Square, Baker Street and some others, so we decided to start the evening down there. When I arrived at Sloane Square, just down the road from the Chelsea flat, there was Philip Sallon dressed to the nines, George was dressed as Boadicea, and I was in gothic robes with green make-up. The usual suspects were there too – Sullivan, Bowen, Jones, Caplan, Franklin, Claire The Hair, Lee Sheldrick. My mum had also come. I'd asked two other friends, Christos and Barry the Rat, to bring ghettoblasters to provide the music and others had brought alcohol to drink in the carriage. By the time we were all together there must have been about 75 of us. When we started to get on the train, London Transport sent a warning out that some freaks had taken over the train. As the train pulled out of Sloane Square we cracked open champagne, toasted our success and drank our way around the capital. We stayed on the train, drinking, until we reached the next pub. But when we got to Baker Street, guards were waiting to meet us off the train. When they saw us, it was as if they'd seen a horror movie. They didn't really know what to do because we weren't really breaking any laws.

After we had been round the Circle Line a couple of times, we got off the train and headed for Hell. It was a great night, but one thing really sticks in my mind. It was the night that I introduced my mum to my boyfriend Ian B. He was about six years older than me and a very famous model – an Armani regular and one of the first male supermodels. We had initially made eye contact at Blitz, but it had been made known to me that the boss of his model agency was his lover. Infatuation on both sides overtook us however, and eventually we both decided we didn't care.

We'd been together about three months by then. But mum just looked straight through him. She couldn't acknowledge that I was bisexual. When I asked her why not, she said, 'You're not bisexual, it's just the people you are hanging around with in this world.' Mum always wanted to think that girls coming to the house in Wales were my girlfriends, even when they weren't.

Some of the wicked behaviour that went on at Hell certainly justified its name, and yet Blitz was even hotter. One night, the club was so sweaty we had to open the back doors, which opened out on to a graveyard. That night a lot of people had taken acid, so there we were, people like Billy Idol and the dance troupe Hot Gossip, everybody off their head, tripping on acid, dressed in bizarre cloaks and hats, dancing around this Covent Garden graveyard. It just seemed completely surreal.

Boy George was among the gang, but his days were numbered. George and I were always falling out. One night at Le Beat Route, with my next boyfriend Lee, I'd got up from my seat to go to the bar and get a drink. When I got back, our seats had been taken by my friend Linda Gallagher, and George. I leant over and said, 'If you don't move your fucking legs, this can that is in my hand is going to be in your fucking face.' I would never have done it and, in fact, that was when Linda and I became friends. George said, 'Ooh, Miss Strange has got the claws out tonight. She must have got out of the wrong side of the bed.'

He had been warned about stealing from people's pockets at Blitz, but I'd reinstated George because he said he would not steal any more. Then, one night, the designer Judith Franklin's handbag went missing. I was convinced it was George, but it could not be proved. A posse even went to his squat to search it. Judith was one of our good friends, I later used her outfits in the Mind of a Toy video, and this wasn't on. We couldn't find the bag, but I decided to sack George. To say he wasn't happy about it is an understatement, but then again, it was the making of him. He decided he could do better running his own club, and he and Philip Sallon went off and started Planets. That didn't last long, but then George started to get Culture Club together. So you could say getting sacked from Blitz was the best thing that ever happened to Boy George.

What Rusty and I really needed was a bigger venue. We couldn't meet the demand, but we knew if we didn't expand, someone else would try and take our clientele away from us. Le Kilt, which tried to capitalise on clubland's penchant for tartan, was being run by Chris Sullivan. Chris was a good friend but he too was clearly thinking about branching out. He had tried a one-nighter, as they became known, at the St Moritz club in Soho, playing salsa and rockabilly, and would soon find success running Le Beat Route on Greek Street with my hairdresser Ollie from Smile. (Twenty years on some things never change. I still have my hair done by Smile, though these days Derek Hutchins does it.)

Rusty and I eventually found the perfect place for our next venture: the Barracuda Club at 1 Baker Street. We called the night Club For Heroes. The opening night was a big test. Would our fans follow us, or move on somewhere else? We needn't have worried. The first night was the hottest ticket in town. I remember it well because we decided we were going to promote British designers, which I had always wanted to do as soon as we had somewhere big enough. We had a show featuring clothes by Fiona Deeley, Stephen Linard and Melissa Caplan. To my huge relief it was a phenomenal success. There were 700 people inside and another 700 outside trying to get in. I felt as if I really had the Midas touch.

I always liked to keep an eye on what other clubs were doing. A place I used to check out regularly was the Embassy. Lady Edith Foxwell, who co-owned the club with Stephen Hayter, could never have been more hospitable – any excuse for a party and we would be there. One year, I was invited down to her country retreat in Wiltshire to open the village fête, which was weird. I was standing there in my New Romantic plumage, surrounded by a gaggle of tweedy characters straight out of The Vicar of Dibley.

By now we were attracting all sorts of celebrities. I had got to know

Heather McCartney, and one day her stepfather, Paul, rang me up. He was working with Michael Jackson and asked me if I would look after him. Initially we met up in a quiet, exclusive wine bar in South Molton Street. When I met him, he was with a much older man who you would have thought was his grandfather because Michael, who was in his thirties then, was like a ten-year-old boy with a girl's high voice. He kept calling the man 'gramps'. He asked for everything in a whisper. You could see by his behaviour that he had never been in a normal environment. When he came to Club For Heroes everything was 'amazing'; he sat there, fascinated, saying, 'These people are so wonderful', as if he was in Disneyland. He couldn't take his eyes off everyone. He was looking at them as if they were storybooks. Then, after a while, he decided to dance. That was when he blew everyone away.

One night, Joan Collins turned up with her third husband, Ron Kass. At the time, Joan was a huge star, both for her soap acting and her roles in the Cinzano television adverts. I showed the couple to their table, and went to get them some champagne. I decided to open the bottle myself, which was a terrible mistake. The cork popped and the champagne squirted all over Joan's face and her dress. She gave me a look of thunder, then, after a moment, she laughed and said, 'Steve, you could do better than Leonard Rossiter in the Cinzano adverts any day.'

Around this time writer Molly Parkin, who lived near to me in Chelsea in the Rolling Stones' house in Cheyne Walk with her daughters Sarah and Sophie, had taken me under her wing and had started penning very enthusiastic features about me. She was also Welsh, which may have been part of the reason why she championed me. It was a spooky house because Keith Richards had moved out, but the house was unchanged. There was even a shrine to Jimi Hendrix. One night we were returning from a party at the Embassy, and Molly was very drunk. I was worried that the taxi driver might try to take advantage of her, so I stayed in the cab to see her home. I remember taking her in and, as we were walking through the hall, she said to me, 'Steve, turn out the lights and I'll take my false teeth out – you'll never know the difference.'

The more coverage our clubs got, the more the media tried to pin a label on us. But we changed so fast it was impossible. Every week the clothes would be different, as people constantly tried to outdo each other. One week I'd turn up in a bishop's outfit, the next week I'd be working on the door dressed as an adult version of Little Lord Fauntleroy. Somehow though the term New Romantic seemed to stick and I couldn't really argue with it.

Without trying, or even knowing what we were doing at first, Rusty and I had kick-started a whole new movement, the first original subculture to come out of England since punk.

CHAPTER FIVE

POP LIFE

As New Romantic bands started to form, it was time to re-enter the pop fray. The demo tapes had gone down well with both clubbers and record company executives. It had been a lucky break to inherit the free studio time from The Rich Kids, but we were determined to capitalise on it. Midge, Rusty and I decided to get a proper band together.

We looked around at other bands who were doing similar music to us and approached like-minded musicians. One natural ally was Billy Currie, who was the keyboard player in British electro-pioneers Ultravox. Then there was the band Magazine, who had been formed by thinking man's punk Howard Devoto and were now on the verge of disbanding. Dave Formula was their keyboard player and Barry Adamson their bass player. With Midge on guitar, Rusty on drums and myself on vocals, we were a real band at last.

Everything was becoming serious now. Our management company, Morrison O'Donnell, saw the potential of us as a proper band. Chris Morrison and Chris O'Donnell were my first managers. At the time, they handled Thin Lizzy and also Midge. They were a very good team. Their company was called MOD, and I was personally looked after by a man called Martin Barter. My public relations person back then, Tony Brainsby, was great too. Tony died a couple of years ago, but I owe a lot to him. He had some great parties at his house in Edith Grove in Chelsea, where I got to know people like Bob Geldof and Steve Harley from Cockney Rebel. It was also at Tony Brainsby's house that I first took cocaine. Tony was a veteran of the rock scene, and drugs were an ever-present part of the lifestyle back then. It was easier to accept them when they were offered than constantly to say no.

Through Tony and the two Chrises I got to know Thin Lizzy's front man, Phil Lynott, better, although Phil and I had already met through hanging about at the Speakeasy and through Phil's wife, Caroline Crowther, who was also a friend. When Phil Lynott took time off from Thin Lizzy to release his solo album, Solo in Soho, in April 1980, he mentioned me on the track Talk in 79, in which he sang about the way the new wave of post-punk music had taken over, alongside bands such as The Clash, The Police and The Boomtown Rats: 'Steve Strange began to change.'

Phil and Caroline were always great fun to be with. I can remember going to their wedding party at the Hilton in February 1980. It was common knowledge that Caroline's father, the entertainer Leslie Crowther, did not really approve of Phil. But at least he showed a glimmer of a sense of humour during his speech, when he recalled Phil asking for his daughter's hand. He said, 'You've had everything else, you might as well have her hand.' I think there was an element of humour in the Chinese theme for the reception – the lanterns and dragons everywhere certainly gave a different meaning to the drugs phrase 'chasing the dragon'.

I came up with the name of Visage. 'Vis' stood for the visual elements of the band, 'Visa' represented the fact that we were going to be a global band, and 'age' symbolised our part in a new age of music. We started to work with the producer Martin Rushent, who had done a lot with electronic bands and would later make the classic album Dare with The Human League. I remember going to his studio outside Reading, which wasn't quite finished at the time. It didn't look like anything more than a shed in a rather large garden. Yet some fabulous music came out of there, and not just ours. We would work in some great studios later on, but nothing was quite the same as Martin Rushent's Genetic Studios. Martin worked closely with Midge, who would be very strict with me. If I was off-key or got the wrong notes,

I had to do it over and over again. But I didn't mind, because we were all trying to make the best album.

Our first single Tar, about the pleasure and pain of nicotine, came out on 7 September 1979, before we had our proper long-term record deal. Martin Rushent helped us by putting it out on his own Genetic Records label, through Radar Records. The only trouble was that Radar's major label distribution deal collapsed soon after release, making the single hard to obtain and, as a result, a collectors' item. It was nice being a cult, but it would also have been nice to sell records, so with the finished album under our cummerbunds, we set about looking for a better deal. Polydor was the lucky label, but it took over a year before we could release our next single.

Having selected Fade to Grey as the first Polydor Visage single, to be released on the same day as our début album, 10 November 1980, we had to shoot the video. The Ashes to Ashes promo had cost £50,000 – the budget for ours was only a fraction of that. With the directors Kevin Godley and Lol Creme I came up with a storyline for the video in which make-up came to life and changed my body. My eyebrow turned into a snake, and my arms were painted like snakeskin. My arms went round a girl, played by my friend from Blitz, Princess Julia, making her arms become snakes. Then my arms became a snake, the snake bit me and I died and faded to grey.

Coming up with the idea for the clothes after meeting Melissa Caplan and Stephen Jones, was one thing, but then we had to film it. It was a long, hard process. I had to shave my whole body to be painted at the beginning of the day's shoot. I was painted silver, and scales were painted on my arms – it was all very intricate. It was hot too, standing around all day covered in greasepaint. At the end of the day, I had to rub myself down with a Brillo pad and turps to get the paint off, and I was totally knackered. A lot of work goes into making a three-minute pop video.

It was funny that Julia had to mime the French lyrics in the song, because nobody could have been less French than Julia Fodor. She was a real cockney and had a lovely voice. You'd hear her saying, ''ello darling y'alright, everyfinks going OK.' She sounded dim, while, in fact, she was actually really bright. Like the rest of us, she would never leave the house without putting on 'the face', an evening ritual that had to be done to perfection. When we worked together at PX we'd be clubbing all night and sometimes go straight into work after a three-day stint of partying. I look back and think, 'How the fuck did I manage that?'

With the help of the striking video, the single quickly took off. It eventually reached number one in nine countries and number two in the UK. In Germany, it was number one for eight weeks. But there was one thing that did piss me off in a big way. We always wrote as a five-piece band, with the lucrative publishing royalties being split between us equally. Someone might come up with a lyrical idea and someone else might finish it off, so the fairest way was to share things. Even if one of us wasn't in the studios one day, the credits were shared. Maybe I was naive, but when the record was released, my writing credit was left off Fade to Grey. The final credits, unlike other songs on the début album, were Ure/Currie/Payne. Chris Payne was a member of Gary Numan's band. He had worked on the song during soundchecks on Numan's 1979 tour, when the song was originally called Toot City. Even though I hadn't come up with the actual lyrics, it had been my idea to do some of them in French, so I had certainly had some creative input. And the concept of the award-winning video had been my idea. I was the face of Visage, and yet my name was left off the writing credits for our biggest hit.

It was even more annoying because when Fade to Grey came out I was the one who was immediately in huge demand. I have always liked to keep myself occupied, but I had never been so busy. The trouble was that unlike most bands, Visage wasn't the kind of group that could go out on a live tour to promote their records. We were essentially a studio band at this stage. When it came to promoting ourselves, there were the videos, of course, but the burden of responsibility fell on my shoulders. I was the focal point of the group. Journalists weren't interested in speaking to the other members; TV shows weren't interested in interviewing the other members. Even if a pop programme wanted a 'live' appearance, it would be me who turned up to mime to a playback. For all the hard work promoting Fade to Grey that was the thanks I got – being left off the writing credits was like a knife stabbed through the heart.

When Fade to Grey was a hit, Rusty and I moved to a place just off the King's Road, a very nice flat in Chelsea Manor Gardens, just round the back of the Town Hall. It was open house for people from the clubs and it would often be crowded with people coming and going. The Chelsea flat was where Boy George met Kirk Brandon, who was the singer in Theatre of Hate. Kirk had been going out with a friend of mine called Jenny, who ran a fifties retro stall called The Girl Can't Help It. I introduced George to Kirk when George was round at my flat, and I said I was just popping over to the shop to see Jenny. George came with me, Kirk was there and George immediately fell for him. Not surprisingly, Jenny instantly hated George. She was a big Scottish girl from the Gorbals, who could have put a guy out with one punch. Maybe she sensed what was going on as she shouted, 'Get this transvestite out of my shop!'

I had a great time at the Chelsea flat. There was only one incident that really spoilt it and that was when we were burgled. I woke up one morning and went into the living room. I noticed that the video and the television were gone. I didn't think a great deal of it because I just thought that Rusty had taken them into his bedroom to watch porn videos with whoever he had picked up that night. I went and had a shave, and then went into the kitchen to make breakfast. It was then that I noticed the front door propped open with an empty beer glass. I thought maybe Rusty had popped out, but when he hadn't come back after 15 minutes I knocked on his door. There was no answer, so I looked inside. He was there, completely dead to the world, fast asleep. There was no woman in there. Or TV. Or video. I woke him up, 'Rusty, what have you done with the TV and video?' He said, 'What do you mean?' Princess Julia was living there at the time too, so I went into her room and asked her what had happened, and she didn't know either. The scariest thing was that when I went back into my bedroom, I realised that the burglars had been in there while I was asleep and had tried to remove the stereo, which was attached to the wall. Looking round, we realised other things were gone too. They had got in over the roof, through the patio window and out the front door. It was always scary coming back to the flat late at night after that. You never knew what might happen to you.

Around this time my itinerary went mad, I was leaving the house at 6.30am to get to Paris at 10am, then leaving Paris at noon, getting to Germany at 2pm then checking into a hotel for two hours, having a snack and a shower, then off somewhere else, maybe a couple of TV shows in Italy then back to London. I didn't have any time to think for myself. I was just driven from one appointment to the next.

I didn't really object to all the travelling at first. Up until this point, the only time I'd flown before was on a school trip to France. It seemed exciting to be picked up in a limo and to travel first class and stay in the best hotels. But I was naive. I thought everyone in the pop business was treated like a porcelain doll. I really didn't realise at the time that it was only being done for me because I was making the record company so much money, and that as soon as the hits dried up, so would this kind of treatment. Furthermore, no one ever explained to me that the money this pampering was costing was actually coming out of my own earnings. I thought I was being spoilt, but I was actually paying for it all myself.

But in the end there were just too many interviews. Not just press, but TV and radio too. It got to a stage where I started to think, 'Did I just say that to the last interviewer, or did I just say it to you?' And when you are working, you don't see anything but hotels, parties, night clubs and TV studios. You'd see the same faces wherever you went. I met Freddie Mercury and Roger Taylor, whom I became friends with, and in Germany I'd see Nina Hagen, whose records we had played at Billy's. Sometimes I'd be doing the same shows as Spandau Ballet or Duran Duran, who had started to take off by now. I might bump into Grace Jones and go to a party with her.

The demands on a pop star are huge. I did wonder how I could manage it all, but then I found the answer. Wherever I went cocaine was always on offer. It didn't matter which town I was in or even which country, there always seemed to be an accommodating dealer on hand, cutting up lines of white powder. It was the kind of drug that would give you a boost to get you through the next round of interviews or television appearances. It was as much a part of the music industry as a guitar and drums. I suppose I didn't see it so much as a cocaine addiction, more as a way to keep me going at the pace at which I had to work. But as the schedules got more gruelling, the dependency got greater. There was never really a chance to recover.

I hadn't taken drugs very much since my Wigan days. At the club I used to drink heavily, but that was only to give me Dutch courage. I may have seemed confident, but I used to drink to get over the initial awkwardness of walking into a room and all eyes being on me. It banished the fear. It seems innocent now, but until Visage took off, drinking to excess was the only way we abused our bodies. Spandau, Boy George and the rest of us were a posse who liked nothing better than to get plastered. I was never a beer man, it was Bacardi and coke – Coca Cola – until I graduated to vodka and tonic.

By early 1981 my workload could not have been more hectic. Visage had grown beyond anyone's wildest expectations and I was constantly being invited to do photo spreads, interviews and public appearances. Fade to Grey had been a hit and we had stolen a march on the rest of the New Romantic scene, getting our début album out long before Spandau Ballet released theirs. There was always an element of friendly rivalry between us. We didn't mind the others doing well, as long as we did better.

It was a nice feeling that we had pipped Spandau. I remember them coming to the playback of our self-titled début album because their producer Richard Burgess had worked with us on some of our album too. They nodded in encouragement, but you could sense the rivalry. They would have liked to have beaten us to it, but they had to wait until March 1980 before Journeys to Glory, their very own New Romantic manifesto, was released. Instead the first lines you heard on our album seemed to be the motto of the movement: 'New styles, new shapes, new moulds: that's the role my fashion takes.'

In fact, it was Richard Burgess who was one of the first to use the phrase 'new romantic'. Soon it was noticed that the visual flare and fondness for historic styles of the Blitz was also shared by the piratical look of Adam and the Ants and Bow Wow Wow. New Romantic seemed to sum us all up neatly. It was certainly preferable to being called glam-rock revivalists or the Now Crowd.

Polydor was keen for a second single to be lifted from the album and we chose Mind of a Toy. Once again we asked Godley and Creme to put across my ideas for the video. As the song was about childhood it made sense for me to use my Little Lord Fauntleroy look. At the start, you see me as a little boy, then as I walk through a magnifying glass my age changes, while my clothes stay the same. I put the magnifying glass to my lips to make them huge, then to my eye which makes it a doll's eye, lending the promo a creepy, haunting effect. I turn into a porcelain puppet and I'm controlled by strings that are attached to my arms and legs. Then at the end I turn into an old man, sitting on the stairs, reminiscing, while massive licorice allsorts tumble down all around me, children's dolls come to life and chase me and a doll's house goes up in flames. Maybe it was too effective. The video was banned by Top of the Pops because they said it was frightening for children.

I suppose if you were the pretentious type you could say the video was all about my relationship with Polydor. Sometimes it felt as if they were treating me like a puppet and pulling my strings. The single was another huge hit and Polydor were still happy, so the whole charade of limousines and hotels carried on. I was no longer a free agent, able to sort out my own affairs. My agents, Morrison O'Donnell, put my business diary together and it seemed to take up every minute of the day.

There are certain important things about being famous that the music press never tells you. When you are hot, everyone wants a piece of you, and, although I was a huge success, I was still pretty green. I was asked to be in a film called Pommi Stern, over in Germany. I didn't stop to find out what the film was, I just said I'd do it because I thought it would help to promote the records. I'm sure it was dreadful. I played the part of a rock musician who has a long-time girlfriend who also wants to be in the music business. Knowing the bad side to the industry, knowing the false promises and the bad directions and temptations, I was supposed to protect her. I wish I'd taken some of my character's advice myself. The one thing I knew was that I was not an actor back then. It was supposed to come out at the same time as Fade to Grey to help to promote the single in Germany. In fact, by the time it came out, the single had already been number one and it was the hit Visage single that ended up promoting the film.

At the same time, I had a club to run. Club For Heroes was really taking off. The celebrities all queued up to be seen. There were people like Kim Wilde, David Van Day from Dollar, Marc Almond, Spandau and even older musicians such as Phil Lynott and Pete Townshend, who had become a good friend of mine.

Pete had come to the opening party and was back the following week. I noticed him going into the toilet and he asked me to go in too. I wasn't so naive by then, it was obviously to do some drugs, but I was too busy to join him. He was taking ages and I kept watching to see when he was coming back. After a while I got a bit worried. I went into the toilets and knocked on the cubicle door. There was no answer, so I called security, who kicked in the door and found Pete on the floor. He had passed out, so they put him in the recovery position. I called for an ambulance and Pete was taken out on a stretcher. He was a genuinely lovely man, but at the time he was a heroin addict. I realised later that I had saved his life, but at the time all I was thinking about was that no one else must come into the toilets and find him like this. It was a very frightening experience. I nearly had a heart attack myself. Drugs were starting to appear on the club scene around then. It was a bizarre time. I hadn't taken heroin, but it was becoming quite fashionable. I thought maybe it was slow-down time, but that didn't happen.

There was a brief period at the beginning of 1981 when I ran a club at the Venue opposite Victoria station on Thursday nights. I had been able to put on some pretty big bands such as Depeche Mode, Duran Duran and The Stray Cats, but it didn't really have the right atmosphere. Half the audience dressed up, but the other half seemed to come along to gawp at them as much as see the bands. I was always on the lookout for a way to make clubbing different. In March 1982, with a girl called Yellana, I set up the Sterling Club, which was very inventive for its time, at Kensington Roof Gardens, off Kensington High Street, which had been the famous Regines in the seventies. It was a place to go after Sunday lunch, where you could sit down and read a Sunday paper, have afternoon tea, play backgammon, chess or card games. You could feed the pelicans in the garden, be entertained by a drag act or a comedian or novelty act, then the bar would open and there would be a DJ. The music was unusual too, mingling Visage and Spandau Ballet with the Sound of Music or Jungle Book in a way that became avant garde. The DJ at the time was Jeremy Healy. These days he is one of the most famous DJs in the world, but this was his first-ever job. It gave clubland a new boost. It was also quite intense. Because of the strict Sunday licensing laws the bar was only open from 7pm to 10.30pm, so people only had three hours to get pissed.

When the third single, The Damned Don't Cry, was released in February 1982, the promotional treadmill was more hectic than ever. Midge had seen how Godley and Creme worked, and wanted to direct the video himself. We shot it at Tenterden station in Kent where we were able to hire a steam engine and a Pullman carriage to recreate a romantic 1930s atmosphere. The only trouble was that it was so cold while we were shooting the video that the diesel froze in the catering truck, and when we broke for lunch we couldn't get any food and we were absolutely starving.

We were trying to recreate the mood of the Orient Express. The whole video was supposed to be this surreal dream, as I go through different carriages and see ghosts appearing. At one point, I see a party going on, but only two people there are real, the rest turn out to be mannequins. In the buffet car, the barman offers me a drink, then turns out not to have a reflection. I can remember the shoot well, because in the middle of it I had a call from my PR Tony Brainsby to say the paparazzi were after me because they had heard that I was having a whirlwind romance with Kim Wilde and we were going to get married. I found it all highly amusing since all that had happened was that the previous night we had had dinner together. It was probably Tony Brainsby himself who leaked the story to get some publicity for my new club, the Playground.

The Lyceum just off the Strand was closed and we told the owners that we could fill it, but they would have to invest a lot of money in the decor. We went for a hi-tech industrial look. Every Saturday we would arrive early, build stacks of scaffolding and pile banks of television sets up at the side. The place had a unique futuristic look and it soon filled up. It was a short-lived club but a fantastically successful one.

It was when I went around the country to promote the single that it really hit me how successful Visage were. In May I had to fly up to Glasgow to open the new branch of HMV Records. I turned up and there were 3000 screaming girls outside the shop. It looked like there was going to be a riot if I didn't appear. I came out, got up on the counter and started dancing, when suddenly there was this almighty crash. Windows started getting smashed and the police had to be called. I became a shopkeeper's worst nightmare. I finished my appearance and then had to get out of there as quickly as possible. I was dragged through the crowd, thrown into the back of a white stretch limousine and given a police escort to the airport. It was terrifying. The car could barely move because of fans trying to climb on to the bonnet and even on to the roof. All I could hear was the pounding of angry female fists on the windows. At the same time there was something euphoric about all the attention. It does give a strange boost to your ego.

My life had completely changed. I couldn't leave the house on my own and I had to put on my full make-up just to pop down to the shops. I had become public property. One day in the street someone looked at me and said, 'Cor, mate, you're not on stage now!' So I turned round and said to him, 'My dear, I'm on stage 24 hours a day.' Quentin Crisp would have been proud of me. I was attracting so much attention I had to hire bodyguards. My old mate Jonathan James, a strapping rugby playing friend from Merthyr Tydfil moved up to London and I didn't dare go anywhere without him. His father was the local undertaker so he had built up his muscles as a lad carrying coffins.

As well as moving to a bigger club, I was looking for a bigger home. The lease had run out on the Chelsea flat, but I found the perfect residence a couple of miles away at 26 Kensington Park Gardens. My tastes had changed a lot since my squatting days. The rent was £450 a week which didn't seem like a lot. I was eating at Langans, having my photograph taken by David Bailey for the cover of *Ritz* magazine, and with his wife Marie Helvin for the Valentino advertising campaign. One night, over dinner, David Bailey introduced me to the photographer Helmut Newton, one of my all-time favourites. I needed a place with style to match my status. This was a grand four-storey house owned by Johnny Stewart, the main Russian artefacts expert at Sotheby's. Johnny was a colourful character whose family owned half of Scotland. He'd be suited and booted for work, but he rode a huge motorbike and in the evenings would wear leather and hang out at gay clubs.

I rented the penthouse flat while the actor Oliver Tobias rented another flat there. The house was decorated from top to bottom in Sotheby's furniture. The whole place was covered in period decorations. There were Edwardian gilt chairs, Persian rugs, mirrors from floor to ceiling. My bedroom had an *en suite* bathroom, a four-poster bed with the most luxurious of silks and antique tapestries on the walls. Johnny's own collection of priceless icons covered the walls. I didn't even know what an icon was until I moved there. I thought it was a pop star. It was completely over the top, but perfect for me. Johnny had a butler and we shared an au pair. How things weren't stolen when I had so many parties there, I don't know. Only one icon was gone when we left and a few plates were broken, but that was about it.

Moving addresses didn't stop hassle from fans. One day I did a photo shoot for the German magazine *Bravo*. Some German fans saw the feature and when they were in London they tracked down the house. One morning after a heavy night, I stood at the window, wearing just my pants, to open the blinds – and all these screams rang out.

There was a coach load of German fans outside. The article hadn't revealed the address, just said it was near Notting Hill, but there was a picture of me on the balcony looking out over the road, and they had tracked the house down by walking around the streets and looking for the same view.

German fans always seemed to be the most determined. Once, back in Newbridge, when my mum was away, Tanya opened the door and there were three girls there who had tracked me down after seeing a picture of my house in a German magazine. They had come over, found Newbridge in north Wales on a map, gone there, realised it was the wrong one and hitched to south Wales. They tried to find me by asking for Steve Strange, and had even looked for my nan in nearby Oakdale, but eventually thought of asking for Harrington. They came to the house and got no answer because Tanya was working nights. My neighbour Alwyn, however, told them it was the right house and invited them in out of the cold, fed them and put them up on the sofa. Tanya has a heart of gold and when she got home and met them, she let them stay there. They ended up meeting me outside a television studio in London. They got a kiss and an autograph, but I could only spare about 15 minutes. That was the kind of madness that went with being a pop star.

Kensington Park Gardens became known as the place where there would always be an after-hours party. Anyone who was in town for Top of the Pops would stop by. It became like Paddington Station. It was here that the cocaine really started to flow. I was using so much and sharing so much out that I had a courier permanently on stand-by to collect fresh supplies from my dealer. We had a prearranged code. One telephone call and the supply was immediately topped up. I don't know how I was never busted. Anything could happen there. One morning I woke up and Robert Palmer was next to me in bed. That was the night that some guys didn't have all the luck. Then again I didn't want the luck.

The stunt motorcyclist Eddie Kidd was also around Kensington Park Gardens at the time. Eddie, who is strictly heterosexual, was convinced that Marilyn was a woman. Meanwhile Marilyn was convinced I had the hots for Eddie, and was really jealous when I was alone with him. In the end Eddie gave Marilyn a lift home and I don't know what happened after that...

Oliver Tobias was a bit older than me, but he was rather partial to younger women, so would sometimes come out on the town with me. One night I decided to go along to Tramp with Oliver, Princess Julia and an old punk friend Wendy Tyger. I was dressed like an extra from a Clint Eastwood movie – complete with quiff, cowboy boots and spurs, and I remember being on the dance-floor with Wendy giving it our own version of Hot Gossip with a sexy dance routine. She had her legs around my waist and was writhing up and down my body. In Tramp, people never stand up and applaud you for dancing, but then suddenly everyone was going crazy. I kept giving it some more, until suddenly I realised I was standing on my own. Wendy had disappeared. I graciously continued to dance and then walked off to my seat. Five minutes later Wendy stormed back to me, 'You could have told me that my bloody two-piece had come apart.' The reason the whole place had gone berserk was that her leotard had opened up and she was showing everything she had!

Despite my mother's disapproval, my relationship with Ian B had been a happy one. I was lucky that my management never insisted that I say I was strictly heterosexual in interviews. I didn't make a big deal about being bisexual though. I'd just say I was sitting on the fence. I might have been going out with a woman but if a good-looking boy took my attention the door was always open. As with David Bowie 20 years earlier, the blurring of the sexual boundaries was all in keeping with the flamboyant character I had created.

If I found someone attractive, I found them attractive and it didn't matter to me what sex they were. In the past there had been casual relationships with both men and women. With Ian it was a particularly complicated relationship, because if his boyfriend had found out about me there would have been trouble. At the beginning of the relationship we were discreet, staying in a lot, but towards the end we would go out more together and we were more honest and open, appearing together in restaurants and clubs. I didn't really care who knew about my sexuality when I met Ian. People around us certainly knew we were an item, but as it became more widely known, it became more difficult for Ian. In the end we decided we had to split. My increasingly busy schedule made it difficult for us to find time to spend together and he was tormented by the prospect of his boss finding out about us. Ian went off to live in America where he ended up becoming a successful actor.

Until then, I'd dabbled, but never fallen in love with a man. When Ian told me he was going, I remember that I'd never felt that hurt before, even though I'd split up with girlfriends in the past. I never felt betrayed, because I knew why he was doing it, but it really did cut me up, so much that I even thought about going to America. In the end I decided I couldn't, because it was another world and would have meant me chucking everything in just on the verge of the boom.

I was pretty heartbroken by the end of the relationship with Ian. On the rebound I ended up with Lee Barrett, a young guy I knew who had recently come out of prison. He had only been in for petty crime; he was just an Essex lad really. I helped Lee out a lot and made him my personal assistant so that he could travel with Visage. Wherever I went in the world, he would come along with me. One of the first holidays I had with the money I made was in the Bahamas. I took Lee, and we rented this fabulous house on Paradise Island. That was where the sexual chemistry started to take off. The trouble was that Lee had difficulty admitting he was gay, and it used to make me so cross. It got to the stage where his denial and my jealousy reached boiling point. When we were back in London it was as if he was embarrassed and did not want to be seen out with me. He couldn't show me any affection and if anyone said anything to him like, 'How long have you been seeing Steve?' he'd reply, 'Oh, we're just friends.' I could have gone out with anyone and I chose him, yet he wouldn't acknowledge me. After a while it started to niggle me and we would have arguments and confrontations. I asked him why he was hiding this, it was as if he was making me out to be a bit cuckoo, as if the relationship was all in my head.

We had a turbulent year together which culminated at my birthday party at the Embassy club. My mum, my aunt, my cousins and my sister were all up in London, and Lee did a very sweet thing, he bought me an expensive camera and arranged for a surprise birthday cake to be delivered. But I'd got it into my head that he was having an affair with a friend, and I said to her, 'Some fucking friend you turned out to be.' I couldn't take any more. It was the final straw. There was a jealous streak in me and whenever my back was turned I thought he was having it off with some woman. I'd taken this for about a year and the night after my birthday party I said to Lee, 'It is obviously not working. I want you out of the house.' It broke my heart but I had to do it, even though I was completely gutted.

About three months later I had a call from Lee, who asked me to come and see a new band called Pride that he was thinking of managing. I wasn't that impressed with the band but I suggested he put the backing singer, Sade Adu, up front. I lent him £5000 and within three months Sade was the hip thing. Soon he was a millionaire and had a house in Little Venice.

Even now I still have a passion in my heart for Lee, I have really fond memories of times with him. There was one night I was doing a TV show in Italy. Perri Lister, Billy Idol's partner at the time, was doing some backing vocals for Visage at the time. After a night of clubbing with Grace Jones we were out near the Colosseum by one of the fountains. We were all really happy and Lee picked Perri up and walked to the fountain. It felt like the perfect opportunity for me to push them both in and give them a soaking. I was just about to do it when they screamed, 'Don't!' I'd almost forgotten that they had all the cocaine in their pockets . . .

With demand for information about Visage coming thick and fast, we set up a fan club, which was run from the bottom room of the house by a friend called John Macdonald. The fan club would receive strange packages addressed to me. I'd get a lot of teddy bears and pierrot dolls, and then there were parcels containing knickers and bras. Every now and again John would open an envelope, particularly from Japan, and there would be a gold bracelet in there. Others would write saying they were the perfect girl for me and then go into details about what they would like to do to me sexually.

While I was in Visage, sex was handed to me on a plate, particularly when I was doing gigs and public appearances. I found it weird. I'd think to myself, 'Do I take advantage?' but I would say no. It was very tempting, but I was worried that if it was only a one-night stand, afterwards they might have contempt for me rather than admiration. Maybe I was tempted a few times, but more often than not I would be too busy thinking of the consequences to say yes.

Maybe it was because we were all young and had far too much energy, but sex seemed to be on everybody's mind. One night Jonathan James and I went to a party at the Embassy club where I got introduced to Hamish MacAlpine, from the wealthy MacAlpine family, and his fiancée Bianca. We went on to Tramp, and Hamish said he wanted Jonathan to do a driving job for him the next day, so asked him to drive him home. They were drinking back at Hamish's and this gay guy called Steven made it clear that he fancied Jonathan, who was completely straight. Hamish said Jonathan should stay the night as he was going to be driving for them the next day anyway, and he was probably already over the limit. At this Steven's eyes lit up.

After Hamish and Bianca had gone to bed, Steven turned up in Jonathan's room – naked, of course. Jonathan wasn't having any of this and asked him to get out. Steven went downstairs, and the next thing Jonathan knew, he was being confronted by Steven and two snarling boxer dogs. Luckily for Jonathan, the dogs started fighting each other, instead of Jonathan, and chaos ensued. Then Hamish woke up, came in and commanded the dogs to stop fighting. After a while, Jonathan and I started to take these colourful events in our stride. Nothing could surprise us.

The success of Visage in England didn't take me by surprise, but the success in Europe exceeded our expectations. I knew that our sound was inspired by electronic music from Germany but our popularity on the continent was still a shock and it meant that I had to perform in front of bigger crowds than I had ever imagined.

Fade to Grey won Single of the Year on Radio Luxembourg. We were driven along in blacked-out limousines to the venue to receive our award. We went under a tunnel right to our dressing rooms so I had no idea that we were in a huge football ground. In fact I didn't even realise that we had won the top award, I thought maybe we were just going to perform the song. There was a lot of waiting around as they called out the winner of the Bronze Lion, then the Silver Lion, then they called out our name and asked me to come and collect the Gold Lion. I walked out on stage and I couldn't believe what I saw. There were 70,000 people watching me. You've got to remember that Visage was never a gigging band so I didn't have any experience of appearing in front of such a large crowd. When we walked out my legs went to jelly. I was overcome by the sheer size. When the announcer said, 'Please put your hands together for Steve Strange,' I walked up to him thinking he was going to give me the award, so I held my hand out, but he didn't give me the award, he took it back and I stood there with my hand still sticking out and shaking in mid-air. I didn't know what to do. I was going to put my hand in my pocket, but then instead I held my hand in the air. As soon as I did that, the whole stadium erupted. It was as if my legs had been given this power boost which took over my whole body. We did two songs, and when I came off stage they couldn't shut me up I was so high. 'That's it, we are going on tour, set the tour up as soon as possible, I've never felt like this in my life, this is amazing, this is the best rush ever . . .' I went on like this for an hour. Cocaine was nothing compared to the first gig we had ever done as a band. The fear was immense but the power rush was truly euphoric.

CHAPTER SIX

TRANS EUROPE EXCESS

After that baptism of fire, appearing in front of a large crowd was usually fantastic. I remember appearing at the San Remo Pop Festival in Italy in the summer of 1982 with The Thompson Twins and Grace Jones, and it was one of my most frightening experiences ever. Rod Stewart was supposed to be headlining, but as show time approached he hadn't arrived. We had all done our rehearsals and we assumed Rod would come later, but ten minutes before I was due to go on stage I was told that Rod was not coming because he had a throat infection. I wondered how the hell I was going to tell 60,000 screaming, hysterical, Italian Rod Stewart fans that their idol was unavoidably delayed? I couldn't even speak Italian. Then, just as I was going on, I realised that Italy had just won the World Cup. I broke the news that Rod Stewart could not make it, and then shouted, 'You should be happy, you've just won the World Cup!' That got them in the palm of my hand.

Travelling around Europe, I'd get to know the other pop stars on the same promotional trail. The second time I met Grace Jones we ended up going on a three-day bender, not to the amusement of the record company. Perhaps, after that, it was no surprise that tempers started to get a little frayed. There was a press conference after the third day, which was when tantrums started to happen and I put my foot down. It felt as if I had been promoting Visage all around Europe for the last year without a break and I needed to release some pressure. After three days of getting in at 8am there was no way I could have done a straight interview, even if I had been awake at 11am. I got a severe telling off.

European television had a habit of testing my patience to the limit, but bad behaviour was not always entirely my fault. We were number one in Italy and we had to do a programme in Milan. I had two backing singers with me, Perri Lister and another girl, Dominique. We were told to get to the studio for 9am to be made up, but I told them that we would do our own make-up so we didn't need to arrive until 10.30am. Unfortunately, we all liked to party and we didn't get in from the previous night until 4.30am. We got to the studio at 11am, but things were running late anyway. It was scorching hot and it got to 2pm and nothing had happened. By this time I was beginning to think that we'd been professional enough. Then they called a two-hour break for a siesta – I always thought siestas were Spanish. I was really fed up and wanted to go, but they wouldn't let us leave the TV studios. At 5pm I went to see the producer and said, 'Can you please tell me what is going on? Why are we hanging around?'

It turned out it was all to do with the singer Sheila B. Devotion. I've never seen anyone with so much attitude and so much unpredictability. At the slightest wrong angle or make-up problem she would click her fingers and call for her make-up artiste and hairdresser. The producer said, 'You need this TV show, just stay in your room.' I said 'Excuse me, we are number one, we don't need this TV show.' We had sold a million albums and had had two million-selling singles, why should I be treated like this? I went back to the dressing room, got the girls and said, 'We're going.' We got the limo to the airport and got straight on a plane back to England. By the time the story got back to England, I was the biggest prima donna going, *so* unprofessional, but this time my conscience was clear. Other times maybe I wasn't exactly in the right...

Because of the growing importance of pop videos, we were able to make an impact in Europe through extensive television promotion. It was hard work, but soaring record sales showed that it was a successful tactic. America, however, was different. It is a huge country to conquer and you have to be there in the flesh to make a splash. We decided to have a go at cracking America, but we certainly weren't going to do a conventional tour. Bands like The Police had made it big there by squeezing into a van and playing every dive from toilets in Tucson to armpits in Arizona. That could never be my style. With my businessman's hat on, I realised that we had to pull off stunts to get as much media attention as possible.

The American promotional tour signalled the beginning of the end of Visage Mark 1. My relationship with Midge had always been a bit fraught. We were like chalk and cheese. He was the studio perfectionist, I wanted to get my vocals done and go. The tension increased the more exposure I got. He had started the band and brought me in, and he was unhappy that I was now getting all the attention. It was understandable, in his past bands he had always been the lead vocalist and now he was having to take a back seat.

Things finally came to a head with the camel. Midge just wouldn't accept the camel. I wanted to cause a stir when I went to New York. We had an appearance planned at the prestigious Chase Park Club in Manhattan. I told Midge I was going to ride down Fifth Avenue to the club on the back of a camel. Midge wasn't keen on the idea. 'If you get on that fucking camel, that's it, I'm leaving the band.' I said, 'Right, fuck you, leave the band then.' I had originally wanted to enter New York on an elephant, but it couldn't be arranged. I was a reasonable man, I settled for the camel. Except that they couldn't get the camel to come out of its truck. It was all very chaotic, but that just made the television coverage even more spontaneous. I knew it would get us coast-to-coast publicity.

Over the next three weeks, my backing singers, Perri Lister and Lorraine Whitmarsh and I made a series of personal appearances across America. I wanted to invite stars such as David Byrne and Andy Warhol, plus midgets, strippers and jugglers to give the evening the feel of a colourful circus, so that every party had a surreal atmosphere. I auditioned the top models around to take part in a fashion show too. New York had never seen anything like it, but the city loved it, even if Midge didn't.

The next day we were due to leave New York for LA, where we realised the same trick wouldn't work when we heard how the Californians had reacted to the camel show when they had seen it on the news. The West coast kids saw the colourful outfits and the antics, and thought we were hippies, just like their parents. In Los Angeles, I wanted something different to arrive in, so I hired a cowboy stage-coach. We had brought in Melissa Caplan and Stephen Linard's designs, and we spent days going through their portfolios to find something suitable for a fashion show. I was doing all the choreography too. Then, at night, there was a lot of tension, so the cocaine came out again to help me perform. That show went without a hitch and we set off around America, staging parties in every city we visited.

Everywhere we went to I came up with a different theme. In Chicago we planned to hire a bullet-proof 1930s car and ride around like gangsters. But we always had a lot of hassle from the American record company who didn't understand my way of doing things. In San Francisco we were met by the classic denim-clad American record company representative at the airport who immediately said, 'I love you guys, I'm really into your music.' It always worries me when someone like that says something like that. I wanted to make the show we were going to do there special, so I went out and auditioned muscle men, tightrope walkers, magicians and fire eaters to perform at the gig and make it feel like a real event.

When we did the auditions, there were seats in the auditorium. I said I wanted them out, 'This is not a gig, it's a party and a fashion show. Get rid of them, otherwise we can't fucking do the show here.' The guy said they would take the seats out. That evening we grabbed a bite to eat and afterwards when the limo dropped us at the venue, it was great to see that there were queues around the corner. It was not great when I walked in and saw that the seats were still there. I found the record company rep and gave him a piece of my mind, 'The seats are still here. We are out of here. You lied to me. You are fucking taking the piss. There's no way this party is going on. People can't just sit there when everything is happening. Why the fuck have you done this? The party can't go on or we will be slammed for this.' He only had one feeble answer, 'Well, they can dance in the aisles.' I'd had enough. I called over the models and the backing singers and we stormed out and got into the car we had hired that looked like it was straight out of an Al Capone movie. There we were, like James Cagney and his molls, being chased by the record company through the streets of Chicago. We got back to the hotel, ordered some champagne and barricaded ourselves into our hotel room.

We could hear them banging on the door, but we just ignored it. We had our drinks and then decided the only thing to do was to go out clubbing. We found a nightclub, which turned out to be just round the corner from the place we were supposed to have appeared. The nightclub would have been perfect for the show. Most importantly it had no seats. The next day, I asked the record company why they didn't book this venue. They claimed it was already booked, which was absolutely wrong because when I was there the previous night I had spoken to them and they had said it was available. They seemed certainly in the wrong, but at the same time the lethal cocktail of success and drug abuse meant that I was becoming increasingly demanding and difficult.

With money coming in from record sales, I started to travel and discover new horizons. I went over to Egypt. The first thing that shocked me was arriving at Cairo Airport and seeing tanks trundling down the street and men everywhere carrying guns. I was horrified. Then, in the city, the soldiers walked arm-in-arm kissing each other. It was all very strange. The trip opened my eyes to another culture – when I wasn't being hassled by sex-mad Egyptian men. They would carry my luggage to my room and then, with a funny look in their eye would say, 'Is there anything else I can do for you, sir?' One day I was in a cab, and when I leaned over to pay the driver, he was sitting there with his cock hanging out. On the whole I preferred the view of the pyramids.

I'd been invited to stay at the Grand Oberoy Hotel. The owner, Bicky Oberoy, was a friend of my friend Lady Edith Foxwell. On the way there, I saw carcasses hanging outside butchers' shops, beggars with limbs missing and poverty everywhere. The contrast with the opulence of the hotel could not have been greater. I remember opening my bedroom doors and all I could see were the pyramids. Bicky made my stay unforgettable, seeing the Valley of the Kings, travelling up the Nile; it was magical and I was determined to go back.

One night, around Christmas, Johnny Stewart asked me to throw a big joint party at the house for both of us and Johnny's boyfriend Edward. I remember it vividly because it was a night when Boy George and I weren't on speaking terms. All the usual pop people were there – Spandau, The Belle Stars, Bananarama, some of Depeche Mode, most of Duran Duran. The party was in full swing. If there was ever a party on the circuit, Philip Sallon would tell everyone, so suddenly we had this whole influx of people, from goths to punks to rent boys to prostitutes. The first person I saw was George, and I screamed, 'Turn that fucking music off. O'Dowd and Sallon, out of this party now, this is my house so I don't fucking want you two in here!' They didn't move, so I literally marched over to them, got George by the scruff of the neck and said, 'Now out.' After that, the party was a big success, although afterwards it was soured when I heard that a friend of mine from Wales, Steven Mahoney, was beaten up on the way home by some people who didn't like the way he was dressed, and he ended up scarred for life.

Soon after I split up with Lee, Francesca Von Thyssen came on the scene. Chessie had become a well known face at Blitz and we had a great rapport. It was a relationship that seemed to suit both of us. She knew I was bisexual but we hit it off really well. She also wanted to be a backing singer and she was able to join Visage and travel the world at the record company's expense. She wasn't a great singer, and never sang on the records. Even live, it took ages of practice before she could lip-synch, but I did it because it was fun having her with me.

Chessie was not your average clubber. She was also known as Baroness Francesca Von Thyssen Bornemisza. She was the daughter of Heine Von Thyssen, one of the richest men in the world, and his wife, the former model Fiona Campbell-Walter. We seemed to have a lot in common. We were both Geminis, both outgoing and outrageous. We both liked to party and our priority was having fun. We liked the same sort of music and had the same circle of friends. Gradually the friendship evolved into a romance.

What I didn't realise at the time was that her father did not approve of me to the extent of having me checked out, I was told later, by the FBI. Her mother, Fiona, could not have been nicer. Inevitably her father must have thought that I was after her for her money, but nothing could have been further from the truth. I just saw her as a soul mate, my perfect girlfriend, not a rich woman. If I had ever have married anyone it would have been Chessie. I never lived off her money, I had money of my own and I didn't mind spending it. My trouble has always been that I would give my last penny away to someone that needed it. Whenever we went out to eat, every bill was shared.

When I told my mum about Chessie, she wasn't rubbing her hands thinking, 'Steven's going out with the richest man in the world's daughter,' but she was pleased and excited. I think it was probably because she hoped I was about to settle down with a woman rather than a man. I never saw Chessie as a pound note either.

Together, we became one of London's most fashionable couples. Stores loved it when they saw us coming. We would go to Vivienne Westwood's shop in the King's Road and empty it, coming home with black bin-liners full of her latest collection. We had a penchant for Yamomoto and Commes Des Garçons – and those suits don't come cheap. Vivienne was very tight with discounts, it was only through my friend Lisa who ran the Yamomoto shop that I got a discount. Sometimes she'd ring me up at the end of the day and say, 'Hi Steve, the takings are down today, could you pop over?' They would close up the shop because my fans would spot me in full make-up and start following me around Knightsbridge. I'd run into Lisa's shop and she would quickly lock the door behind me. Lisa's bosses were incredibly tight though. One day they gave me a present for being a regular customer. It was a filofax. I told them to stuff it up their arse, if that was all they could do after I'd spent £15,000 in their shop. It was different with Jean-Paul Gaultier because I started to model for him and I'd also struck up a friendship with Claude Montana and I was allowed to go into his warehouse and have the pick of his clothes.

I behaved like royalty. I would never carry money. If I saw something

I wanted I would take it off the racks and then send my bodyguard Jonathan around with a briefcase full of cash handcuffed to his wrists to pay and pick up the garments. I had no idea about money. All I knew was that it was there to be spent. I was living a lavish lifestyle, I was taking lots of people out and footing the bill, and I had a big cocaine addiction.

The success of Visage also helped the success of the clubs. I was approached by a huge company called European Leisure, who said they would finance any project I wanted to suggest. That was when Rusty and I came up with the idea of The Camden Palace. The venue, on a busy junction on the corner of Camden High Street, just opposite Mornington Crescent underground station, had formerly been the grotty rock dive the Music Machine. This was long before Camden became chic. You've got to remember that in the early eighties Camden Town was still a fairly grimy place. The market had yet to take off and there were drunks and homeless people everywhere. Winos and tramps would sleep in the doorways and it was almost impossible to get a taxi to pick you up at the end of the evening.

Rusty and I had always been really confident. Nothing stood in our way. We had a go-ahead, suffer-later approach. We didn't ever think that anything we tried would fail, but The Camden Palace was our biggest club yet and maybe, for the first time, I wondered if we had pushed club culture too far. I wanted the venue because it had a capacity of 2,500 and it had huge potential, but before it could open it had to change dramatically. The stage for the bands had previously been right in the middle of the dance-floor. That had to go for a start. The lighting rigs had to be changed around. The balconies were cleaned and the bars were smartened up. The old Music Machine sign came down and the new name, The Camden Palace, went up.

The Camden Palace opened its doors on 21 April 1982 with the slogan, 'A club made by the people, for the people.' Despite the increased size, and the increased number of nights the club was open, business still boomed. Even though you had to take your life in your hands to go to Camden back then, tickets were like gold dust. The area was so crowded, the police had to close the road off. We'd sent out too many tickets, as most promoters do, expecting a lot of people to stay away, but they all turned up. The police had to close down the street because there was so much traffic. But as the stars danced and drank the night away they did not realise what a close-run thing it had been. When I'd arrived at the club at 5pm, the varnish on the dance-floor was still wet.

Mum and Tanya came up from Wales for the opening night too. It was great to see my family again. I'd always tried to stay in touch with them after I realised how much my mum had worried about me when I first went to London. The previous Christmas I had returned to Wales like Santa Claus, with a big sack of presents for Tanya over my shoulder. They were really proud of me. Tanya was delighted to have a big brother who was a pop star. When she came up to London and said she was hungry I think she expected me to buy her a bag of chips. Instead I took her to Langans.

The first night at The Camden Palace was one of the best nights of my life. I did a couple of numbers. Depeche Mode were there, Ultravox were there. The dance group Shock performed. Night Train was just about to be released as a single. If The Camden Palace had blown up that night, half of pop land would have gone up with it. All I can remember about the opening night is breathing the biggest sigh of relief ever.

For the first week, I bit my nails wondering if people would turn up each night. It was as if we had tapped into a hitherto unknown stratum of young people who did not want to spend all night in a pub but did not want to spend all night at a gig either. In sociological terms this was truly a new era. Clubbing had always been around, but until now there had either been the choice of small suburban discos or classy élitist nighteries such as Tramp. This was an altogether different phenomenon. And yet the larger we got, the more people would turn up. I thought the bubble would burst at some point and we would reach full capacity, but I'd turn up at the door and find that Rosemary was still having to turn people away. We could afford to turn people away if they didn't look right because we always knew there would be enough of the right kind of people to fill the venue.

Despite the location, The Camden Palace quickly became the club that everyone wanted to go to and be seen at. Celebrities were as keen on it as clubbers. Sade, one of the original St Martin's crowd, who was now managed by my ex-lover Lee Barrett, did a gig there. Madonna made her London début there in 1983. It didn't feel right, because we preferred to have live bands and she wanted to sing to a backing track, but her manager was desperate. He said that nobody else in London would have her. In the end we put her on and she sang Holiday, going down really well.

If you wanted to stay up late and party, The Camden Palace was king. We turned a pretty grotty rock venue into the most glamorous club in London. For a while I did worry whether we could fill it, but it was an immediate success. The one problem was the doormen, who had not been my choice. They were gorillas in suits, such as the late bare-knuckle boxer Lenny McLean. I didn't like this because I always believed that the first impression you get of a nightclub is the most important one. If your doorman can't even string a 'good evening' together it doesn't exactly create the right impression. There was an added problem with the doormen because when I was tied up with Visage Rusty had asked his girlfriend Hayley to be the greeter. The doormen soon had Hayley in tears. She was scared to answer back to them so they were basically deciding who to let in. I soon put a stop to that and put Rosemary Turner on the door. When she turned up they said, 'We'll soon have you crying like the other one, love,' but Rosemary was always able to give as good as she got. 'No you won't,' she replied. 'I'm from south London and I can take a lot more shit than you can roll out.' They got on very well after she had let them know who was in control. The greeter was more important than ever. At my previous clubs everybody had to pay to get in. I now started to compile a guest list and Rosemary would stand on the door ticking off the names as they entered.

I was always keen to support designers and show the links between pop and fashion. In March 1983 Antony Price staged a fashion show at The Camden Palace, with Marie Helvin and Jerry Hall modelling for him. It's funny to look back on it now. Tickets were only £7.50.

There were some great nights at The Camden Palace. One February we had a St Valentine's Massacre Ball. I went as a gangster and Francesca accompanied me as my moll. Arnold Schwarzenegger, Christopher Reeve, Jack Nicholson, Zandra Rhodes and my mum were there too. Jack Nicholson was lovely. He never forgot me, and more than ten years later he came along and said hello to me when I was running another club in the West End. Sylvester Stallone was very loyal too. He always stopped by when he was in London, and years later when I was asked to relaunch The Camden Palace he turned up and stayed beyond the call of duty to help me get some publicity for the club.

Mum got on famously with the celebrities, particularly Zandra Rhodes, who also turned out to have a house in south Wales. Mum took meeting stars in her stride. One night she came to the club and ended up going out for dinner with Christopher Reeve.

The paparazzi would hang around outside always hoping for a photo opportunity. Sometimes we gave them one just for a laugh. Therese Bazaar had recently been in the papers saying that she was no longer romantically linked to her partner in Dollar, David Van Day. Therese and I appeared together arm in arm and the next thing we knew, the papers were saying we were madly in love. It was just like the story with Kim Wilde. I had a fairly happy relationship with the papers. They may have printed untruths, but they were pretty harmless untruths.

Another bizarre occasion with mum was when a tabloid wanted to do a thing about celebrities and their home towns. Mum came up to London for the photo shoot and that night we all went out clubbing. Phil Lynott gave mum what she thought was a French cigarette but was actually a joint. She smoked half of it and said the room was spinning. At the shoot the next day she felt terrible but had to go through with it. I sat politely at the dinner table in my gaucho outfit, fedora and pants from Melissa Caplan, while mum kept having to disappear to throw up.

One of my allies in the press was Paula Yates. We had first met at a funfair in Berkeley Square. Paula and I had got stuck at the top of the Big Wheel. She ended up being there for so long that she wet herself. We soon became firm friends. Paula had a column in the *News of the World*. I would tell her stories and she would exaggerate them to make me sound sexier, writing things like, 'I'm lying on Steve Strange's four-poster bed and he is standing there pumping iron and really turning me on. He is a real flirt.'

One of my most treasured memories of Paula was our trip to Paris with Martin Kemp. Polydor had put me and Martin Kemp up in one of the best hotels in the city and *Cosmopolitan* had sent Paula out there to do a story on us.

As usual Paula, Martin Kemp and I had been out and about getting seen and snapped. It had been a particularly mad night. We had been invited to a spectacular party for Jean-Paul Gaultier at Le Palace, downstairs at an exclusive club called Le Privilège. As we arrived at the top of the stairs, Martin, the bastard, seized the perfect moment and picked Paula up to carry her. Paula was wearing a beautiful gold lamé dress by Anthony Price and looked fantastic. It was like a lightning storm as all these flashbulbs went off. I was walking behind her and accidentally caught my foot on the hem of her dress. I didn't think I had done any damage, and yet the photographers were going crazy. It was only when we reached Le Privilège that I realised why they were so interested. Paula's dress had unravelled. All she was left in was her bustier, her thong and a bit of lamé covering her modesty. She was lucky she was wearing a thong. Normally she didn't wear any knickers.

I needed a lot of time to recover from the excesses of the evening. We got back to the hotel at 7am, and I gave strict instructions that we did not want to be disturbed until 1pm. Suddenly, at about 9am, the phone rang. I answered it, half asleep, said I did not want to be disturbed and put it down. It rang again. I picked it up, said 'Don't you understand English. Call me at 1pm,' and slammed it down again.

The phone went again. I said 'Make that 2pm for waking me up.' I was just getting back to sleep when there was a knock at the door. I decided I was never going to get back to sleep until I sorted this out, so I answered it and saw these two huge guys with American accents, who turned out to be CIA. 'I think you should listen to us. We have the ex-President of the USA downstairs and you are in his favourite suite, so would you vacate this room right now.' It was decidedly non-negotiable. I said we would move but not until they gave us another room. I knew how hard it was to find decent accommodation during fashion week and I thought they would never come up with an alternative. In 15 minutes they found us another suite, which was fine since we were never there except to shower and go out. When we moved, there was a knock at the door and a magnum of champagne arrived with an apology from ex-President Nixon, who had decided to visit Paris on a whim and always had the same suite.

For two years The Camden Palace was a success. The worst incident that happened there was when I was 'arrested' for possession of cocaine in the toilets. I can laugh about it now, but I was furious at the time. One night in October 1983 I went into the toilet with Eric Payne, who had been doing some work for me. Something didn't seem quite right. There was somebody standing there giving me a funny look. As I went to leave, Eric passed me some cocaine, wrapped up in paper. There was barely enough for one line.

Suddenly Eric and I were grabbed by two men who then pushed us up against the wall and searched us. They didn't find anything else, but they began to frog march us out of the building. I shouted to the general manager, Mick Parker, to stop them, but they flashed their id cards and the next thing I knew we were at the nearby Albany Street police station. Unfortunately Rosemary had not been on the door that night to vet who was coming in, and was not there to come to my rescue when they took me out of my club.

It turned out, however, that they weren't police at all, but a Falklands veteran and a serving paratrooper who were on their very own clean-up London campaign. I wasn't worried about my innocence but I was worried about the bad press for the club and Visage. But at the police station the officers were barely interested. They treated the citizen's arrest as little more than a joke, but reluctantly they had to follow it through. The trouble was that the case dragged on. The incident was in October 1983 and it didn't reach court until October 1984, by which time my involvement with The Camden Palace was over anyway. At Snaresbrook Crown Court no evidence was offered against me and the charge of cocaine possession was promptly thrown out. The judge's attitude was that the police had a hard enough job and these self-styled do-gooders made matters worse rather than better by clogging up the courts.

CHAPTER SEVEN

INTO THE ABYSS

I had ambitious plans for the second Visage album. The Anvil was going to be a no-expense-spared lavish affair, with a launch party in Paris and films shot to accompany some of the tracks. The plan was to shoot a globe-trotting epic, with each different country conjuring up a different mood.

I went back to Egypt to film a video for The Horseman, one of the album tracks. It was one of the hardest jobs I'd ever worked on. The weather was so hot during the day that we had to start at 5am and have hair and make-up ready before sunrise. All I can remember is the hassle involved in getting permission to film on the pyramids and the number of times they had me running up and down these fucking pyramids in a one-off Vivienne Westwood outfit. I would have preferred it if we hadn't got permission. Riding through the desert on a white stallion dressed like an Indian prince was more fun, in fact it was completely surreal. I couldn't shake off crowds of little Egyptian boys who were intrigued by my appearance and fascinated by the way my spiky hair stood on end.

When it came to shooting the album cover, Helmut Newton, whom I had met over dinner with David Bailey, was my immediate choice, and the budget soon began to rocket. My black leather suit alone cost £1,500, a huge amount back then. Then there was the hairdresser, stylist, make-up artiste, the six models all dressed to look like Aryan men, food and drinks. It didn't help that we did the shoot at the George V Hotel, the most famous hotel in Paris. There was my hotel suite, rooms for all the models, stylists, hairdressers and make-up artistes.

We picked up their expenses and they all took advantage of the mini-bars. The two-day budget came to £175,000. It was worth working with Helmut, but maybe it should not have cost that much.

They say you should never meet your heroes, and while I loved Helmut Newton's work, in some ways he turned out to be a disappointment. I wanted to treat everybody well but he didn't care about insulting people. I had hired a private Lear jet to fly everyone over to Paris for the shoot. One of the models was Vivienne Leigh, who had done the recent Cadbury's Flake commercial. Helmut Newton took an instant dislike to her. He was adamant that she was not going to be in the shoot. But I put my foot down and insisted that she should be. One of the girls said, 'Calm down, Helmy, calm down,' and he literally slapped this girl across the face. I was gobsmacked. In the end he added insult to injury by making Vivienne pose as the bellhop rather than as one of the glamorous models in the front.

Second albums often suffer by comparison with the first, and maybe this was the case here. My cocaine consumption was pretty high, and maybe I cared more about the things going on around the album than the music itself. I thought I knew everything. With the first album I was happy to be told if I was off-key. By the time we did The Anvil I couldn't wait to get off to another party, much to the annoyance of the rest of the band. Most of the songs we had rehearsed, but the rest were quickly cobbled together in the studio. We wrote some of the lyrics on the back of envelopes during the sessions. We grabbed ideas from anything we could think of. The title track was inspired by a visit to a New York fetish club of the same name.

To coincide with the release of The Anvil, I decided to stage a big celebration of the best of British fashion in Paris during the spring fashion week. I called the show Motivation, after one of the tracks on the album. I was always keen to champion homegrown designers, and choreographed the show myself. I was able to get the best names together and get great publicity out of our shows. We were basically sticking two fingers up at Parisian couture culture, saying we had the better designers, and Paris was taking the credit for it, stealing our ideas, watering them down and putting the trends on the catwalk. The only French designer that had any originality was Jean-Paul Gaultier. He was pioneering skirts for men, and I adored his collection. I wanted to buy everything.

The British show at Le Palace was a huge success. The five designers represented the cream of British talent: Anthony Price and PX, and newcomers Stephen Linard, Melissa Caplan and Fiona Deeley. It was a sensational show and well received. At the party afterwards I got a message that Rod Stewart was there and that he would like to meet me. It was all very strange. There I was, sitting at the top table, and Rod Stewart, one of rock music's greatest stars, was brought to me. I felt like the king as he leant forward and whispered something in my ear. Would I like to accompany him to the toilets for a line of . . . ?

In the fashion and rock world, drugs were almost a way of life. I was part of that scene too. People weren't exactly coming back to Kensington Park Gardens for a cup of tea. But cocaine had always been my drug of choice. I knew people who took heroin but I had always tried to resist it. By the release of The Anvil, however, I had taken heroin a few times. After that I'd take it about once a month, but I hardly considered myself an addict. I was happy with my life. The band was a success; the club was a success.

And I was making a lot of money. When the first Visage royalty cheque came in, I couldn't believe it. It was for £250,000. I just wish somebody from my management had sat me down and explained that this was not going to go on for ever. I made a lot of money, but the trouble was I spent a lot of money as well. I bought a property in Wales for £125,000 and had it interior designed by Ben Kelly, who had hit the big time and had designed the Hacienda in Manchester. I had grand ideas for a spiral staircase, special plans for customised colour-coord- inated radiators. It was a big waste of another £75,000. If I had left it the way it was, and got my mum to live in it, it would have been better than having it interior designed. My mum lived nearby and I asked her to keep an eye on the builders. All I seemed to be doing was sending them cheques for things like painting, fitting the jacuzzi, doing the central heating ... My mum called me one day and said there didn't seem to be much work being done. I called Ben and he said I should explain to my mum that they were doing work that you couldn't see, inside the house. The house became a millstone round my neck and I ended up selling it for £50,000 when the property market slumped. That money came into my bank account and went straight out again to pay VAT debts.

I had to sit down with an accountant one day. He couldn't believe my expenditure. '£10,00 for a coat?' 'Yes, it's real snakeskin, a one-off.' '£1,500 for a two-piece leather suit?' 'It was for the cover of The Anvil.' In six months alone I had spent £80,000 on clothes. But there's one piece of advice I wish I'd taken from my mum. She'd been out with me when I was paying all the restaurant bills, and she always said to me, 'Steve, why is it that you always pick up the tabs at Langans and Le Caprice. Those places aren't cheap.' I said, 'Mum, they are my friends.' She said, 'They won't be around when things go wrong.' I said, 'Of course they will,' but I should have listened to my mum.

After it all went pear-shaped, most of my entourage soon drifted away. Out of 20 people, around five stuck by me: Rose, Linda, Gabriella Palmona, Wendy and Mark. Wendy also had problems with heroin. After splitting with Martin she had met up with a heroin dealer called Frank, and he was her downfall. Frank knew I had a lot of money and a growing drug problem. If I rang Wendy and he picked up the phone it wasn't difficult for him to arrange to sell me some heroin.

I was earning plenty of money in other ways too, but as soon as it came in, it went out. In 1982 I did a commercial for TDK tapes in Japan, which was on television and on billboards the size of buses. My friend Duggie Fields came back from Japan and said you could see me everywhere. Two tracks from The Anvil, Night Train and Whispers, were used in the ads, which helped to push them up the Japanese charts. They filmed the advert at the spectacular Ludwig's castle in Bavaria, but I don't know why, because when the posters came out, all you could see was a shot of my head, and electricity shooting from my hands and setting the videotape in motion. When the shoot was over

I was given £75,000. Three months later I'd spent all of the money. I thought it would never end.

There was also regular money coming in from The Camden Palace – 2,500 people a night paying £5, six nights a week. The deal was that I took my wages and the rest of the money went into an account called Nightclubbing Ltd that was not to be touched. This account was sacred and no one was allowed to remove money from it under any circumstances. It was for VAT and so on. I had a good team behind me. Carol Hayes, who did my PR for the club, was great. She always made sure that the paparazzi was there to photograph the celebrities at the clubs and kept the momentum rolling. When Harrison Ford or Jack Nicholson came, Carol let the press know about it. The Palace was popular, but it still needed publicity. On Tuesdays and Thursdays we were strict on the door, but the other nights we wanted to attract out-of-towners, so we needed to keep our profile up. I continued as usual running The Camden Palace six nights each week, assuming everything was working normally behind the scenes.

Success had its perks. When I started modelling, Yves St Laurent would send me boxloads of make-up to promote their new lines. I had to laugh, recalling how when I was broke I had nicked bits of make-up. Now I could afford it, I didn't even have to pay for it. The drugs seemed to affect my judgement. I thought I looked great, but others didn't agree. For the Pleasure Boys single sleeve and video I went for a look based on Marlon Brando in The Wild One, but I was no method actor. Methadone maybe, but not method. I posed moodily on my Harley Davidson motorbike in leather jacket and cap, and to recreate the feel of the period we shot everything in black and white. The single, our first track that Midge had not co-written, was released on 5 November 1982, but there weren't many fireworks.

The most memorable moment during the promotion was appearing live on The Tube, Channel 4's new youth programme presented by Jools Holland and my old friend Paula Yates. Unlike most bands, who would perform in the Newcastle studio, we were beamed in direct from The Camden Palace. We did the single, plus the title track from the album. It seemed to go down well, with lasers and a special light show bringing the performance to life. But we were coasting on past glories. After the band's initial impact we would have to make a great third album to keep up our momentum.

During 1983, Visage started to have serious problems. My relationship with Midge had broken down and he had left the band for good. It was that old thing of musical differences, with a bit of ego thrown in for good measure. He wanted to keep to the winning formula of electronic music, while the rest of us wanted to go more rock-orientated. I think there was also the problem that I had stolen the limelight. He had always been a front man, going right back to Slik in the seventies, but the focus was now invariably on me. Maybe I'm wrong, but I think Midge wanted to get some of that attention back, which was why, after the first album, he had started to combine his work in Visage with fronting Ultravox.

In all honesty, I was more than happy for Midge to be the musical brains of Visage. I'm not a person who loves being in a studio. As soon as my work is done, I want to be out of there and off to the next party. Midge would sometimes deplore this, but I always said to him that going to the parties and being seen was helping Visage a lot more than hanging around the studio playing pool.

There were endless meetings about the approach of the group. The problems had started with that bloody camel back in New York. Midge started to get annoyed about what I was wearing, and we would have arguments. Rusty stepped in to calm things down when Midge objected to one of my Vivienne Westwood outfits from her 'nostalgia of mud' collection.

But, at times, there was even friction between Rusty and me over my image. Tantrums seemed to be the order of the day. On one occasion, Rusty arrived at the airport to go to Europe with me for some promotion for the Night Train single. He took one look at me and said, 'You're not going to wear that.' I turned round and snapped, 'Well, you're not going to be the drummer then.' He said, 'You look bloody ridiculous.' I said, 'Keep your nose out or you're not getting on the plane.' In the end he stormed off, and I got a session drummer in for the European appearances.

What annoyed me most, however, was that after Godley and Creme had done a few videos, Midge got it into his head that he wanted to become a video director, and he took over. He did some which were OK, but others that just looked like glorified home movies. They weren't a patch on the creative work that Godley and Creme had done. If it wasn't for Midge, there would not have been a Visage, but I felt I was more responsible for deciding the visual style of the band and he ended up wanting to control that.

I felt that I had gone to a lot of trouble for the band. Not only had I been the face of the band but I had been the one to do difficult things like record a German version of The Anvil, Der Amboss. I had to be coached by a German guy as I read out the words: 'Heisser und schneller'. It took ages, and every time I thought I'd got it right, he made me sing a line again. I was determined to do it, however, as a thank-you to our huge German fanbase. I'd never really enjoyed the discipline of singing, even in English. At the start of Visage I'd had a couple of lessons but I'd soon had enough of singing, 'Bright copper coffee pot'. I wasn't a muso, I just wanted to do my bits and go.

So by the time we set out to make the third album, Beat Boy, this was Visage Mark II. In fact, Rusty and I were the only two original members to stay on permanently. Billy Currie's involvement was limited. Dave Formula only contributed to a few tracks. Rusty and I agreed to be more rock-synthesiser and less dance-music orientated. Without Midge, we felt we could go for a harder edge. We brought in Steve and Gary Barnacle, who were great session musicians, and Andy Barnett on guitar. We began to record our third album at Trident Studios, a place that Rusty had shares in, and we were also able to work on demos at Steve Barnacle's house, where he had his own eight-track studio.

But perhaps the biggest change in the band was behind the scenes. I made the fatal mistake of sacking my original management team, Morrison O'Donnell. I never wanted to leave them, it was Rusty and a couple of the other members saying that this new guy Jean-Phillipe Iliescu could break the band in America. Personally, I didn't care about breaking America, my schedule was hectic enough already. But Rusty kept going on about it and in the end I gave in to him to get a bit of peace. I'm sure my heroin use was part of the downfall of the band, but Jean-Phillipe hardly helped matters. The consequence was that with the next album virtually recorded, there was a contractual wrangle over the tapes. The album took nearly two years to come out – one of the most frustrating periods of my life. You think you've got a good contract, but there is always a clause lurking there that you are unaware of. If we had released the tracks any sooner, our old management would have had more rights over them and we wanted to make a clean break. But the change of management didn't solve anything at all. In fact it made things far, far worse. Apart from taking heroin, that change was the biggest mistake of my life.

So Jean-Phillipe took over. And that was when things started to go in the wrong direction. Rusty recommended him, saying that he had managed bands before and had a lot of good music-industry contacts. But I didn't really like Jean-Phillipe from the start. I just didn't trust him. I had a gut feeling from day one, but after a couple of months, I thought I'd work with him to keep the peace. Soon I realised Jean-Phillipe had even more expensive tastes than I had in my most extravagant moments. I liked grandeur, but he spent money on things we didn't need. Dom Perignon champagne was good enough for me, but Jean-Phillipe insisted on Cristal champagne. He would order caviare for breakfast. And the band paid for everything. To make matters even worse, he moved into 26 Kensington Park Gardens, which was far too close for comfort.

After about a year, Johnny Stewart told me he had had an offer and was selling 26 Kensington Park Gardens. Jean-Phillipe had been there for six months, and I was more than happy to leave. I moved to a house in Hamilton Terrace in Saint John's Wood with my new make-up artiste, Paul Gobell, and Terry Haub.

There were some pretty strange goings-on at Hamilton Terrace. At Christmas, my mum came up to stay with me, and I talked her into letting my hairdresser Peter give her a makeover. Then, on New Year's Day, she cooked dinner for Ronnie and Jo Wood, The Belle Stars, Madness, Boy George and Keith Richards. My mum was in her element cooking lunch for The Rolling Stones. I remember it well because I had started to dabble more seriously with heroin by this point. I would disappear into the bedroom. When I returned Boy George told me off and gave me a motherly lecture about the evils of drugs. At the time he was absolutely against drugs, but he would soon end up on the same slippery slope I was on myself.

Heroin seemed to cause the most unexpected problems. Paul Gobell, who lived in the house, was a larger-than-life, 22-stone American who used heroin. One morning Anne, our cleaner, found Paul naked and unconscious, and couldn't revive him. I'd been on a bender the previous night and she knew not to wake me, but eventually she had to get me up. I managed to revive him, but when he came round he was saying, 'Where the fuck am I?' He was completely lost. We were on the top floor of the house, and the flat beneath had just been taken over by new neighbours. Paul started walking about in the nude, saying, 'I've gotta get a taxi, I'm late for a job with David Bailey.' He strolled into the neighbour's flat, completely starkers, and we had to get him back upstairs. He then passed out, and he was so big that we had to call the fire brigade to lift him up and get him out of the flat. Even they couldn't get him down the staircase, however, because it was too narrow. They had to put him on a blanket and lower him down through the bloody window.

After a while, I moved out of Hamilton Terrace and temporarily moved back in with Rusty in Earl's Court, because Chessie was on one of her jaunts promoting the Thyssen art collection. At Rusty's, Davina McCall would pop around. She was only 16, but she was also a regular on the scene and we had become good friends. She helped out doing flyers for me and would also work on the door if Rosemary was away. Rusty was very anti-drugs. People thought he was always on speed because he talked so fast, but that was his natural way of talking. So while he was in the kitchen tut tutting, I would be in the lounge doing shit-loads of cocaine and throwing his red taffeta cushions across the shiny floor to see who could get them the furthest.

That proved to be a short stay though because I soon moved in with Chessie. She had a lovely place in Seymour Walk, just off the Fulham

Road. The parties continued, with the fashion world mingling with the pop world. You'd walk in and there would be Bow Wow Wow, Chris Sullivan and his wife Holly Hallett, and Lesley Wiener, the first supermodel. I'd just discovered an unknown model called Yasmin, who ended up marrying Simon Le Bon. One evening we were having a barbecue in the garden and people were doing the Double Dutch, the latest skipping craze. All of a sudden this milk bottle came flying through the air over the wall and hit Holly smack in the face. She had to have stitches but it could have been a lot worse.

You never knew what was going to happen at Seymour Walk. After a night at The Camden Palace, Siouxsie from The Banshees came back. We spent all night doing cocaine and chatting. By sunrise we were still up and we started talking about our mutual record label, Polydor. Siouxsie told me stories about her band's relationship with the label, and I said that I'd never actually been to the London offices. She had been with the label longer than Visage, and was horrified that they had never introduced themselves to me. She said we should go straight over there and sort things out. So, on the stroke of 9am we marched into Polydor. They looked at us as if we were martians out of our heads on cocaine, as if to say, 'So, what's new?'

But Chessie introduced me to the real jet set, people like Rolf and Gunther Sachs. It was another world. I remember once we were skiing in Gstaad with Nick and Julie Ann Rhodes. This was at the height of Duran Duran's success, and Nick was complaining that he couldn't get over the fact that he was being recognised all the time. I turned around and said, 'Nick, if you took your make-up off while you were skiing no one would take any notice of you.' Nick always put on a show. I remember being invited to his wedding at the Savoy. Everything was going to be pink, Nick wore a pink Antony Price suit and they even had pink flamingos brought in for the occasion. Chessie couldn't make it, so I took Sabrina Guinness. I arrived in a mauve smoking coat and mauve velvet suit, Sabrina was in a similar colour. We were told to go to the back entrance and when we got there there were hordes of Duran Duran fans. When we got out of the car they were screaming like mad, and Sabrina was absolutely terrified, but once inside we had a marvellous time.

Chessie got on fantastically well with my family. Mum and Tanya came up to stay, and Chessie could not have been more hospitable. In fact, her brother Lorne had the house next door and Fran gave my mum the key, telling her that any time Lorne was away she was welcome to stay there.

It was after we moved in together that we did a lot of travelling together. We were invited to play elephant polo in India, which was positively surreal. There was a team of Indian aristocrats, a team made up of the British Olympic decathlon team and a team of celebrities, including Barbara Bach, Ringo Starr, Billy Connolly, Chessie and me. We obviously thought it was some hilarious joke, but it was very serious out there. We all got on well, but it is hard to play elephant polo when you are pissed every night. When we arrived at the palace, we were put inside these luxury tents and then taken to a party before the first tournament. We were greeted with a bar lined up with eight rows of ready-made Bloody Marys. By the time it came to getting on our elephants, we were absolutely useless. From there we went on to Kathmandu, which was a breathtaking experience. I was transfixed by the clothes and the jewellery, and they gave me a lot of ideas for clothes and videos.

We had some great times in Africa too. Through Chessie I met the Cunningham-Reids, who owned the hotel on Lake Navash in Kenya. The lake was famous for the flamingos that would land on it *en masse* and turn the surface pink. It was like something out of the colonial 1930s; we slept in hammocks, covered in mosquito nets. Everything was unforgettable. I looked at the Masai warriors and incorporated some of their styles into later looks for Visage.

After that, we went on safari, staying in the famous Treetops hotel. We stayed in tents which were pitched around the grazing areas of rhinos and elephants. Because of the wild animals it was dangerous after nightfall. If you wanted to move around at night, you had to get a Masai warrior to take you to the dining room or the bar. To be honest, I didn't think it would be interesting, but when you see the wildlife just 20 yards away from you, it is the most amazing experience. To see a cheetah kill is unforgettable. We went on a hot air balloon safari before sunrise, going where the wind carries you and looking down on the plains, covered in herds of wildebeest, elephants, hippos, crocodiles, landing in the middle of nowhere for a champagne breakfast.

After a while we set off for the island of Lamu, nearby. The record company had given me a set of Luis Vuitton luggage as a gift and as I left the hotel my bags seemed really heavy. As I went to pick them up to walk over to the private helicopter, Mr Cunningham-Reid said, 'Sssh'. He had told his wife he had stopped drinking, but had hidden five bottles of vodka in my bags.

Travelling with Chessie always meant staying at the best places. She was such a well known member of high society that whenever we arrived somewhere, news soon got around and she would receive invites for receptions with the local movers and shakers. They all wanted to be seen with her. In India I did get a bit upset because Indian men seemed to see her as a sex object, and it was as if I didn't even exist. They were all after her.

Chessie and I did everything in style, sharing the costs. If there was a problem, it was that I would have liked to have done the same trips as a backpacker. We went round India one year, staying in Hilton hotels. I suppose it was what Chessie was used to, but I always thought maybe I would go back and do it my way one day. In fact, I recently went to Goa and bummed around, and that was just as much fun and a lot cheaper.

Koo Stark had become very friendly with us around this time. She was seeing Prince Andrew, and they were always trying to avoid the paparazzi, so we helped them out by inviting them to rendezvous at Seymour Walk. It was the perfect location. It was a cul-de-sac, so it was impossible for snappers just to drive past. It was all very cloak and dagger and great fun. There was a special code to inform us by phone that Prince Andrew was on his way. On one occasion I remember the paparazzi was waiting outside. We had a collie at the time and pretended to take the dog for a walk, all the time eyeing up every car and van in the street in case it was a photographer. We couldn't take a risk of Koo being spotted, so we would smuggle her out the back way over neighbours' walls. We even had a decoy transit van waiting outside the house to put the paparazzi off the scent.

One weekend when Chessie's family was away, we all decided to spend the weekend at their house in Gloucestershire, which was an enormous mansion full of great works of art. We avoided the pho-tographers by having two different black BMWs with blacked out windows. Meanwhile, Prince Andrew was on the floor of the transit van. When we were in the clear he joined Chessie in the car. It was all very exciting. Not even the three-mile driveway, FBI and Rottweilers roaming the grounds, and barbed wire could stop a photographer in search of the million-pound photo. One publication had two heli-copters circling above us one weekend. They took it in turns so that there was no chance of missing something when on the ground refuel-ling, but we knew the grounds were impenetrable because the Von Thyssens always insisted on absolute security. The best they managed was a picture of Andrew with a coat over his head.

Chessie and I were very happy together most of the time, but towards the end of our relationship we did start to argue. One night we had a row about whose house it was and I flounced off, saying I would be gone for a week. I ended up coming back a couple of days early and I didn't have my keys. I rang the doorbell and a man answered. I thought his face was familiar and I wondered if I knew him from a club. I said, 'I live here,' and he said, 'You must be Steve. Hi, I'm Michael.' It was Michael Douglas. At this point, Chessie came down the stairs. She was wearing a lilac basque with matching stockings, stiletto marabou mules and a see-through dressing gown that Michael had clearly bought her because I'd never seen it before. This was the first time there was any jealousy in our relationship, and it was a strange atmosphere. We all sat there watching television and I sulked, refusing to make con-versation while Michael stayed around.

Eventually our relationship came to an end. There were too many things wrong. We were too different. It wasn't that our friendship had come to the end of its run; I think maybe the reins were being drawn in by her father. Although I tried to keep my heroin problem a secret, and always kept myself clean and tidy, Chessie found out about it and that started to drive us apart.

We stayed friends for a while, but then she moved away from London. In 1991 she married, and became Her Imperial and Royal Highness the Archduchess Karl of Austria. Her husband's great-uncle was the Archduke Franz Ferdinand, whose assassination in Sarajevo in 1914 started World War One. I was slightly upset that I wasn't invited to the wedding, until I saw the press coverage and realised that very few people from her London life had been invited. She had also moved on from people like Koo Stark, heiress Sabrina Guinness and impresario Michael White. It was as if she wanted to draw a line through her past and start again.

Life, at this time, was made up of great highs and great lows. Due to contractual problems, work on the third album was taking longer than expected, so to pass the time I did some modelling for Jean-Paul Gaultier in Paris. At the after-show party there was a big British contingent: Stephen Jones, Kim Bowen, my friend Steven Mahoney from Wales. It was a scrum to get in, even if you had tickets. Gaultier was the most innovative designer at the time so everybody wanted to be there. As I was leaving the party, somebody asked me why I was going so soon. I said I was tired and had run out of coke. They said, 'Come with me' and they gave me some white powder. I thought it was coke, but when I took it I immediately threw up. Once the sick feeling had gone, however, it seemed to take away all my problems about Jean-Phillipe and the band. About 20 minutes later I asked what was in the cocaine, only to be told that it wasn't cocaine, it was heroin. I was furious. It was a club, it was dark, I didn't know what I was taking. Looking back, I suppose I thought I could keep my heroin use to a minimum, but the problem escalated. It was only in Paris that I realised I was addicted. Until then, I'd only ever chased the dragon, heating up the heroin in a piece of tin foil. This was the first time I had snorted it.

Once you've had heroin, you've got to be very strong to turn it down. It's like a devil nagging you all the time, and when you move in circles where people are taking it, resistance is futile. I had got to know Pete Townshend at Club For Heroes, and in 1982 we had ended up working together. Pete was also dabbling with heroin, but he was a lovely, kind, caring man and concerned about my drug use. He tried hard to impress upon me how bad it would be to get addicted, and I guess he knew what he was talking about. At the time, I was taking heroin, but I still felt I could function without it. It wasn't a daily dependent thing, but a recreational drug.

Around this time, we did some recording at the Townhouse Studios with an androgynous woman in a trouser suit called Ronny. She recorded her own single If You Want Me To Stay, and then we did a cover version together of The Lady Is A Tramp. I thought she was great, but a lot of people thought she was just a copy of Grace Jones. I think maybe she had a bit too much attitude. She was very Parisian, very stuck up, but actually a very nice person. In the video, I wore a specially made corset and dress by Anthony Price and a white wig from Savile Row. Because Ronny looked like a man, I had to play the part of the woman. In the end, the project was shelved, but I'm not sure if working with Pete was such a good idea. He had a heroin problem and if I'm completely honest I suppose I started dabbling in heroin more regularly around then.

My heroin addiction really started when I realised my pop career was on the slide. I think that's the same with a lot of people: Boy George, Marilyn, Ben from Curiosity Killed the Cat. Heroin is like a false security. It makes everything all right when it isn't. George couldn't deal with the comedown of not selling so many records. Neither could I. But George was the person you'd least expect to get involved in drugs – he was always having a go at me and others for taking them and yet eventually he became hooked too. That's how addictive heroin is. In the pop industry nobody ever teaches you how to cope when it goes wrong. I never had a problem with cocaine, I could always function without it, but with heroin you soon can't get out of bed without it. It makes you feel like you are king for the day, when you aren't. It gives you delusions of grandeur and it lets you push your problems to the side, which ultimately makes them worse.

I thought heroin was the way of coping with my problems and all the pressures. Instead it nearly killed me and ruined me financially. Over the next four years I would blow over £100,000 on the drug.

CHAPTER EIGHT

COLD TURKEY

One night after a big party at The Camden Palace I decided I had had enough of this dependency on heroin. The days of hanging around with Pete Townshend and Phil Lynott, and doing it as a recreational drug had long gone. I realised that I always felt sick, my bones ached at every joint and I had no energy at all. I felt the need to get away from London. I never classed myself as a junkie because I didn't use needles but I suppose I was kidding myself. Call it what you like, I was now a heroin addict. The only place I could go was the place where I had my happiest memories. I went to my mother's house in Newbridge to make a clean break and clean up.

I arrived there with no medication. My plan was that some clean, wholesome living would simply flush the addiction out of my system. I had no idea how hard it would be without medication. On the first day I arrived home mum was really happy and I was too. But I remember feeling tired early in the evening and went to bed at eight o'clock, telling my mum I was exhausted.

I woke up an hour later with the most horrendous pains, and had to run to the toilet to vomit. I vomited so much that there was nothing left in my stomach. I desperately didn't want my mother to know what was going on, so I took a bowl and a towel back to the bedroom, where I continued to throw up.

By midnight there was nothing coming out except for green bile. One minute I would be too hot and the bed clothes would be soaking, the next minute I'd be freezing cold. I laid down on my bed and curled up in the foetal position, waiting for the agony to end. I thought that it would go on for ever, until I died. It was unbearable, and at five o'clock in the morning I could not keep the problem to myself any longer. I called out to my mum for help. But I still couldn't face telling her about my addiction.

My aunt was a doctor's receptionist at the time, and I knew what to do. I asked mum to pop round to Carol and ask her for some pills called DF118s. This was an opiate that would stop the cravings and the pain. I will never forget the look on her face, but I didn't want to tell her, I just said, 'Mum, please get them.' She went off in the car for what seemed like an eternity. This was the reality of cold turkey. Mum came back with the pills, but by this time they couldn't help me, as whatever I swallowed, I immediately threw up. After four days I could not stick it any more, and ordered a taxi. I headed for the station and returned to London. I was soon back on the same path again – being clean for a week, then relapsing, hanging around dealers, hour after hour. I seemed to spend most of my time in Mornington Crescent because most of the dealers lived around there. It had always been convenient when I was going to the nearby Camden Palace, I could stop off there and they would set me up for the night. When the people who knew I was on heroin saw me nipping out just before the club opened, they would joke, 'Steve's shopping again.' I guess you don't realise what you are doing, how much you are hurting your friends when you are in that situation.

I can still remember my mum's face now. I put my family through so much worry. I've always said to people that no matter how you get involved in heroin, it is like having a devil on your back, not just the money you go through but the misery you cause everybody else.

Heroin is a horrible thing. You can get over the sickness and the detox, but psychologically there is a power within you that drives you to it even though you know you have gone through so much hell to get away from it. It's the voices that get to you. I'd say to myself, 'I'm not a weak person. Why can't I get this fucking voice out of my head?'

People who had known me before my success tended to stick by me. They could see I had a serious problem and wanted to do something about it. One night, Martin Kemp and Steve Norman rang me up and invited me round to dinner at Steve's house in Finchley. They said to be there at seven for dinner at eight, but that was not what they had laid on. They had decided that the only way to get me off heroin was to lock me up until I was clean. His old girlfriend Wendy had been an addict and had cleaned up at a clinic in Victoria, so Martin knew what addiction and withdrawal was like with medication. He also knew it was worth it even without medication. They held me prisoner for ten days, during which time I went through the same agony of cold turkey that I had gone through at my mum's house. They would take it in turns to bring me my meals even though I couldn't keep anything down. I was projectile vomiting and missing the bowl, but they cleared up my sick and kept my room clean for me. The cold sweats would soak my bedclothes. You could wring the liquid out of them. Martin and Steve would sort the sheets out and make me have a hot bath which took away some of the ache. Even Martin's mum did a shift to look after me. I couldn't phone anyone or see anyone else. Eventually they called in a Harley Street doctor to provide me with medication, and paid the bill themselves. It cannot have been easy for them to see me this way, yet they did it for my own good. It was one of the nicest things anyone had ever done for me. Yet when they let me out, I showed my thanks by going straight back down the heroin road again. I was just not in the right state of mind to say 'enough is enough'. Even when I was clean, I still had those voices in my head. At the end of the day I had to acknowledge that no one can help you except yourself. You have to be the one who says you have had enough, that you don't want it to go on any longer, and that you want it to stop.

Just before this time, I had invited Martin and his future wife Shirlie Holliman from Wham! out to dinner. When the bill came, I said I didn't have enough money to pay it, and asked them for £25. But instead of using it to pay the bill, I went out and scored some heroin. Later on, after Martin and Steve had tried to get me off heroin and I had betrayed their trust I wrote to them and asked them for their forgiveness. Writing the letter I cried my eyes out. On heroin my emotions had been numbed, but now I realised how good they had been to me. I think they were touched when they read my letter. But at this moment things were really starting to unravel. As much as I tried to clean up, heroin addiction was becoming more serious, and times were changing. My involvement with The Camden Palace came to an end when they decided that they could get just as much business without me.

Visage was not doing as well as it had been. We had had hit singles off The Anvil, but they hadn't done quite as well as the early singles. Maybe I realised Visage wouldn't last forever. Around the summer of 1984 I started to get involved with the growing business of styling. I was working with photographers like Chris Duffy and David Levine, and we decided we should set up an agency supplying not just photographers but stylists and hairdressers. We called ourselves the Creative Workforce Team.

One of the first jobs was a swimwear shoot for the *Mail on Sunday* colour supplement. I decided I would champion Yasmin – this was before she married Simon Le Bon. She was just what I wanted for the shoot. It was close to the Olympics and I wanted to do it round a pool, so we shot it at Porchester Baths in Bayswater, which still had the feel of the 1930s. Yasmin was the centrepiece of the shoot, with gold medals hanging off her chest, and boys in swimsuits draped over her. When the spread came out, the *Mail* commissioned me to do a monthly slot.

I moved back into Hamilton Terrace, which became party central again. I decided I wanted my bedroom to be like a bat cave with black and grey walls, and black linen, so that whatever time it was, it felt like night-time to me. Sometimes I lost all sense of day or night. There were times my maid couldn't wake me up and would panic. For the first time I was becoming unprofessional and missing appointments. When I did turn up, I would make unreasonable demands. The drugs made me erratic and a bit of a tyrant, but without heroin I couldn't function. The dealer has what I called 'powder power'. They love to keep you waiting, knowing the agony you are in. It is sheer hell.

When the third Visage album, Beat Boy, was about to come out I decided to take a trip to Paris to see Jean-Paul Gaultier's new collection and to prepare for another promotional round. I had always had my suspicions, but it was then that I finally realised there was something wrong. When I went to leave the Hotel Place de la Concorde I tried to pay my bill with my American Express card. To my horror, my card was refused. I rang my accountant and for the first time I asked him to transfer some money from the Nightclubbing Ltd account into my current account. This was the business account that should never have been touched. I couldn't believe it when he rang me back and said that there was hardly any money in the account to transfer. I was convinced that someone had been siphoning money off. Luckily, I managed to spot an English model, Claire Atkinson, walking through the hotel. Much to my embarrassment she bailed me out and paid my bill. Being an old friend, she knew she could trust me.

Visage was not exactly in its healthiest state at the time, having gone through countless line-up changes. When we had started off everything had fallen neatly into place. Now it had become a struggle. At the beginning we had so much momentum behind us that having our first hits had felt easy. Fade To Grey was the first New Romantic single and everyone wanted to buy it. It seemed to glide into the charts. But four years on that initial excitement about the band had diminished. There were new colourful, stylish bands out there stealing a march on us while Visage was tied up in contractual knots. Spandau Ballet had made it into the mainstream in the summer of 1983, having a number one single with True. And after years of dreaming of being a big star, threatening to be a big star and plotting to be a big star, Boy George really was a big star. Karma Chameleon seemed to spend most of autumn 1983 at the top of the singles charts. It was on the radio everywhere. And these other bands had taken a leaf out of Visage's book, always coming up with a striking new visual image for the videos to keep the television shows as well as the fans interested. I still thought Visage could stay at the top – we were certainly in demand in Europe – but others that had landed record deals after us had certainly made up a lot of ground.

I was so angry, I stubbornly stayed in Paris, but eventually I realised I had to go back. I spoke to Jean-Phillipe on the telephone and agreed to promote the new album on one condition: that there was a dealer at the hotel wherever I was staying while promoting. If he had been a good manager, he would have said, 'No, you are going into the Priory,' but he agreed to my terms. I was stupid. I felt like the king of the castle because I thought I had got my own way, but actually I was more under the thumb than ever. He knew that if heroin was involved, I would agree to anything.

The promotional tour kicked off, but it was a fiasco, and the album got mixed reviews. Bernie from Polydor must have been an angel to put up with me. I was a monster. We were doing record shop signings and I'd be late, or some nights, if the dealer hadn't come to the club, I'd be going through hot flushes and cold turkey. Jean-Phillipe should have put me into rehab, not pushed me out on the promotion trail. But it wasn't the normal Steve Strange that the public was used to seeing. There was a price put on my head by the tabloids so I put my hands up and admitted I was a heroin addict. I tried to explain that it wasn't cool and that I didn't want any of my fans to copy me.

I felt terrible though because previously in interviews I had denied that I was still on heroin. I hated lying, so I decided it was time to come off and I checked into the Priory, which was not anywhere near as well known or well established then as it is today.

To be honest, I found the Priory very money-orientated. It felt as if they wanted you there as many nights as possible. They tried to put me on a drug called Naltroxone, which was supposed to block the effects of heroin, and then they put me to sleep for five days, but once I came out of detox that was the end of their help as far as they were concerned. And because I didn't have any sort of medical or psychiatric help, it wasn't long before I was going to meet a dealer. If one dealer was caught I would soon find another one.

I managed to stay clean for about three weeks, but it was just too easy to relapse. I wanted to get off, but heroin is a demon. When you are busy, you are fine, but the moment you are on your own, you think about it and you want to score.

Somehow, during this madness, I managed to have a relationship with Rachel Byrd, a beautiful model. I had seen her at parties, but I thought she was with someone else and off limits. Then I booked her to star as the lead hooker in the video for the Love Glove single. She was going out with the singer August Darnell at the time, but it was obvious that we fancied each other. In this video the American club personality Diane Brill, dressed in a rubber outfit designed by Daniel James, played the madame who looked after the girls. The scene was shot on the docks, with the sailors eyeing up the prostitutes. Diane had to protect Rachel's character because she was so virginal. It was so cold that when poor old Diane sweated inside her rubber suit, the sweat immediately froze and turned to ice.

At the end of the shoot, Rachel and I exchanged numbers. After she'd split with August Darnell we started to see each other. I even took her back to Wales to meet my mum, who really liked her because she was happy to muck in and do the dishes. Even though we were both grown-ups, my mum didn't want her to stay in my bedroom in Porthcawl. She had to sneak down the corridor in the middle of the night to join me. It was at the height of the miners' strike and I arranged a raffle to raise money for them. The prizes were Simon Le Bon's shirt, Freddie Mercury's trousers and one of my gold discs. Rachel was always happy to help out for a good cause. One Christmas, she joined me, The Thompson Twins, Bananarama and numerous other stars when we visited University College Hospital and various foster homes. We travelled on the back of a carriage pulled by shire-horses, and handed out toys. We knew it would never be a serious relationship, but we had great fun while it lasted. It took my mind off the other problems in my life.

After my nightmare with Jean-Phillipe, I wanted out of the music business, but a friend of Chessie's realised that my real problem was heroin, and introduced me to Smallwood Taylor, the managers of Iron Maiden. They said that if I could sort out my heroin addiction and clean up, they would take me on.

I was really determined to make it this time. I went into rehab again and managed to stay away from heroin long enough to put a new band together. I got Pete Barnacle in on drums, his brother Steve on bass, his other brother Gary on saxophone. I got a girl called Wendy Wu who used to be in The Photons to sing harmonies with me. I called up

Steve New, an old friend who had been the original guitarist in The Rich Kids, to be lead guitarist. He was another ex-addict trying to sort himself out.

My new managers arranged a showcase gig with EMI Records. I didn't really want to sign with them because I remembered how badly they had treated The Rich Kids, giving up on them when their first album failed to top the charts. They came along, anyway. Unbeknown to me, Steve New was an epileptic, and halfway through the gig he started to have a fit on the floor in front of me. Both EMI and my manager said that if the band was going to get anywhere, he had to be sacked. I felt terrible about it, but the way it was put to me was that it was 'him or me'. EMI saw the new band as a touring band and didn't feel Steve would be up to it.

Reluctantly I agreed to do it and we got an EMI deal. I optimistically called the new group Strange Cruise, but I think from that moment my heart wasn't in it, particularly when they sent us over to Germany to a recording studio not far from Nuremburg to record the first album. I used to call the studio the Hammer House of Horrors. We were working with Mike Hedges, who was a good producer, but I didn't like the way he worked. The band, who were very experienced, actually knew more about music than he did and he could not come to terms with it. He liked to mould bands; he wasn't used to musicians with an authoritative approach.

Nuremburg was the biggest disaster ever. The album had the potential to have been a good album, if we had had a different producer. Mike Hedges had done The Banshees and Soft Cell, so he was obviously talented, but we just didn't click. It was stalemate: we were locked into a contract with him. It was winter, an hour's drive from anywhere, snow everywhere.

I hated it there and flew Rosemary over to relieve some of the boredom and stress. I'd try to escape as soon as I knew the vocals were done. I'd get someone to drive me to the nearest town and go out for the night. During the sessions, Freddie Mercury had his 40th birthday party in Munich, and he invited me there. It was like a masquerade ball, the theme was black and white, the whole of the club was decorated in black and white. A lot of the white was cocaine. There seemed to be white powder everywhere. It took three hours to get there and three hours to get back but it was worth it.

The one good thing about being in the middle of Germany was that I was away from heroin. I'd managed to stay clean for about four months and was feeling stronger, but I hated the fact that I would have to pack my things and prepare to go home and start the campaign to promote the first Strange Cruise single. Rebel Blue Rocker was released on 24 February 1986. We unveiled the new band at the Hippodrome in Leicester Square. My mum and my sister Tanya came along to give me moral support, but it would have needed a lot more than moral support to make Strange Cruise take off. After all the problems we'd had in Germany I sensed that things weren't going to work out for the best. The single failed to make even a minor dent in the charts. I'm not even sure if it ever left the pressing plant. Strange Cruise sank before it was launched. EMI barely put up any posters to advertise it. I think we were looked upon as a tax loss, but Iron Maiden were signed to EMI and their management had persuaded us it was for the best. For the video, we wanted to come up with a striking idea. I went up in a hot air balloon over Maidstone in Kent. Unfortunately it was too windy and we were blown off course. The balloon crashed into some oak trees and I hung there for two hours before firemen could rescue me. Maybe it was not the best start to my new band. My career was also veering off course at an alarming rate.

I was getting into other scrapes too. It seemed as if I was attracting trouble like a magnet. One night a group of us went out for a Chinese meal on the King's Road. There was Rosemary, her boyfriend Julian from a band called Das Psycho Rangers, some others and another couple, Julian and Jo. After a while, and too many sakis, there was just Julian, Jo and myself left. We were sitting there for an eternity, waiting for the bill, when someone suggested we should leg it, just for fun. We ran out of the restaurant and suddenly we could hear these Chinese voices behind us. We looked around and the waiters were waving meat cleavers. The joke was not so funny now. We were ducking and diving behind cars and bins, trying to get away. Eventually I got back to

Rosemary's flat. Julian was already there, but Jo was gone. After a while, we drove back to the restaurant and as we went past we could see the waiters holding Jo. After about 15 minutes of deliberation, Julian and I decided we had better go back, just in case they had cut Jo's head off! We walked in very sheepishly and were immediately pinned up against the wall. We got our cash out as quickly as we could and apologised profusely. They let us go, but warned us not to come back again. We were lucky to get away without the police being called. In fact we were probably lucky to get away with our limbs still attached.

With the album not doing as well as past releases, the money was not coming in in such large amounts as it used to, and I had to scale down my standard of living. I moved to a place off the Fulham Broadway, which was more grotty and out of the limelight, but ironically it proved quite handy. Boy George, who had always had a go at me about heroin was now an addict himself and was being pursued by the media wherever he went. He used to come to my house and we would arrange for a dealer to come there to supply both of us. I suppose dealers saw us as an easy touch. Thinking back, I was crazy letting George come round. He had the world's press after him and to get to me without being noticed he would climb over walls, crawl through bushes and through people's back gardens. But then, that's what addicts do for heroin. I never rang him, he always rang me. I didn't think I was helping him, but I knew what he would be going through if he didn't score. I knew the pain of not having heroin when you are an addict.

One day, he was completely out of it. I don't know what he had taken, but this was when he was wearing all those 'fuck you' badges. He was picking up things in the supermarket, throwing things about. A man in there recognised him and the paparazzi were there in five minutes. Luckily George was on his way round to me by then, but the press was in hot pursuit. We had to get him out over the back garden fences. I was offered an absolute fortune to break the story that George was a heroin addict. When David Levine, one of the photographers from the Creative Workforce, did break the story that George was using cocaine, I questioned whether he was doing the right thing. I still don't know if he did the right thing, but George didn't speak to David for the next eight years.

What I do know is that heroin causes nothing but problems. One night in April 1987, I was doing a one-off appearance at Tokyo Joe's, a club opposite the Ritz. When I got back home afterwards, there was a knock on the door. A voice said, 'It's the dealer with some stuff.' I ignored the voice. I thought it must be the press. They said, 'It's for real, it's the stuff you ordered earlier.' I said, 'You must have the wrong house, try two doors up.' I walked away up the stairs, and the next thing I heard was, 'Boof', the door was being kicked in. I turned round and they must have thought I was going to attack them, because before I knew it, I had a gun put to my head and a voice was shouting, 'Where's the money, where is the fucking money? I'm gonna kill you.' I was pushed down on the floor, I felt a blow to my head and I felt blood running down my neck. I was terrified because I didn't know how badly I was injured. I didn't know if I'd been stabbed or just hit. I shouted to my friend Sarah Hoden, who had come back with me, to phone the police. One guy ran upstairs and got Sarah to lay face down next to me. I said, 'There's no money here,' but they started turning the house upside down, asking for my drugs. I told them there was nothing there. Eventually they grabbed some things, a leather jacket, a camcorder and a video and went, but it was absolutely terrifying. I had to be rushed to St Stephen's Hospital, where I had to have stitches. But in some ways the mental shock was worse than the physical injury.

I was traumatised for a while after that. Someone on the drugs scene must have thought I was bringing club takings back to the house, which I never did. I always put them in the safe at the end of the evening so that it could all be banked the following morning. The police came and gave me a real gruelling because they thought maybe it was drug-related and that I had a major supply in the house. I played dumb because I had never sold drugs. At most there might have been a gram of cocaine. The police got nowhere. They fingerprinted the place, but nothing was made of it. I think somebody was involved who knew what I was doing that night, and the money that had been made. Either that, or it was somebody who had been to the house selling me drugs who gave them a tip off, or was in on it themselves.

After that, I didn't feel safe going back to the house. I thought I would be a victim again. The stress was too much for me. Combined with my addiction, I felt I had hit rock bottom. I'd cut all my ties with The Camden Palace, I'd left Smallwood Taylor, I now left the Creative Workforce Team. I didn't know who to trust. The worst thing was the worry I caused my mum, my sister and everybody else in my family who was dear to me. Now that mum knew I was an addict, she was constantly concerned about me.

All I knew was that I needed to get away from London to get away from heroin. At one point I was so desperate I contacted Lee Barrett. He was having huge success with Sade by now and I just wanted some money to finance a trip away. I had never asked him to return the money that I had given him when he went into management, but now I asked for a favour in return. His reply was like a dagger in my heart. He said he couldn't give me the money, because it would be killing me. He thought I would spend the money on more heroin and he would feel too guilty if I killed myself. I cried my eyes out when he said this. I didn't know what to do. I was lucky though. Sade herself heard about my problem through Andrew Hale who was in her band and seemed to understand my need. One day a courier arrived at my door. She sent me a thousand pounds with a simple message, 'Please don't do anything stupid with it. I hope you use it for what it is intended for.' Which was basically to get me out of the country.

Out of the blue something good finally happened. I had an offer to host some nights at the Ku Club in Ibiza. It was just the job. I could get away from all the things that were dragging me down in London, and in particular, heroin. But there were still a few loose ends which had to be tied up first.

Just before I went to Ibiza I was having a thing with Helen De Barge, which ended up very messy indeed. Now I'm streetwise. I'd wheeled and dealed, but I'd never got into fraud and credit card fiddling, that was not my bag.

We had been quite close. She had come to stay at my mum's house and my mum thought we should settle down together. Later on, however, I realised that she had stolen old photos of me from the house, which could have been damaging if used in the wrong way. They were just pictures of me in my punk days in Nazi gear, wearing swastikas, but they could have been interpreted in the wrong way. One day, when we had an argument, she threatened that I would never be able to get rid of her because she had things that incriminated me. At times, it was a difficult relationship to say the least.

One night, after a party at Limelight, a group of people came back to my house in the Fulham Road. In the morning, when I was clearing up, I found a filofax belonging to the PR man for the Limelight, James Ghani. Helen also saw it and when we realised that his cheque book and credit card were in it, Helen, who also had a drug habit, suggested we used it to get some money to buy drugs with. I didn't really realise what we were going to do, but we went along to the Royal Bank of Scotland in Notting Hill and, lo and behold, before I'd really thought it through, I had written out a cheque. I got away with it twice, stealing £300. It was only when I went back and wrote out a third cheque for £90 and handed it over that the cashier asked me to hold on a minute. I wondered if she had recognised me and realised that the name on the card was not my real name. My stomach was getting tighter and tighter. I said to Helen we should just go, but she was too concerned with the fact that we could buy three and a half grams of heroin with the cash.

While we were standing there, a policeman came into the bank and asked to speak to us. He asked me if I was the person who had signed the cheque. I made out I was who the cheque book said I was, but they took me and Helen off in a police car. We were put into cells in the basement before questioning. I couldn't believe I had done something so stupid. As I sat there, a familiar tune could be heard in the distance. Every time an officer walked past my door he sang the chorus of Fade to Grey.

I was interviewed and admitted that I had done it, but had never done it before. Apart from anything else, I was embarrassed because this wasn't a stranger's cheque book but a friend's. As soon as I got out of the cell, I rang him and apologised. James was great and forgave me, but that wasn't the end of the matter. Two weeks later I had to appear at Marylebone Magistrates Court. I told the court that the mixture of alcohol and medication may have affected my behaviour. The judge said that I may have been drunk when I stole the cheque book, but I had certainly sobered up by the time I went to the bank. I was fined £500 for theft, deception and attempted deception, but worse than that was the telling off from my mum who came up to support me. That was when I realised I wanted Helen out of my life, and that was when the pictures came out in the argument. But I had to get rid of her whatever the consequences. It got to the stage where I ended up packing her bags and putting them out on the doorstep. She left, but she still kept returning. She would say we were made for each other and that when she was gone for good I would regret it for the rest of my life, but I just had to make the break.

CHAPTER NINE

THE KU CLUB CLAN

After the failure of Strange Cruise, I didn't want to work in the music business again. I was beginning to realise that I had to do something different; it was either that or take a gamble and start up a regular London nightclub again, rather than just doing the occasional one-off. I'd frequently be asked by promoters to kick-start their clubs. When the legendary Café de Paris reopened I was asked to launch it by the owner. I had my birthday party there and Rosemary Turner did the guest list, which gave the place a boost. People like Andy Warhol and Mickey Rourke came when they were in London. And I finally found room to squeeze Mick Jagger in after the incident at Blitz.

There were new clubs all over London. Rosemary had impressed people so much she was headhunted by the nearby Limelight Club. I went down there and got to know Don Mackay, who ran it. At his flat in Mayfair I met Kevin Spacey, who was over in London doing A Long Day's Journey Into Night – which sounded a bit like my life story. We met up with the co-stars Jack Lemmon and Peter Gallagher and went off to dinner at the Groucho Club. I was getting by, but I still had the heroin addiction hanging over me. There were too many temptations in London.

Initially, I thought I was being a coward by just running away to Ibiza, but the offer was too good to miss. In London, the dealers seemed to have an infallible homing instinct, and as soon as they knew where I was living they would be knocking at my door. Everything was too intense. Boy George had heroin problems of his own and would be knocking at my door begging to come in to score some heroin. The only thing I could think of was to escape to an island. Back in the early eighties, Ibiza was unspoilt. Once you got away from the club areas and the bustle of the port you could switch off. It was the real jet-set island with annual concerts by all the big bands from Queen to Spandau Ballet. I was there once at a party for Elton John and his manager John Reid, who stormed out and got straight on his jet because his suit hadn't arrived. I was no angel there myself. I ended up being caught taking cocaine in the room where, unbeknown to me, a writer from the *Daily Express* was staying. The journalist was furious and tried to get me thrown out. It was a decadent, hedonistic place, but best of all for me, there was ecstasy and lots of cocaine but, at that time, no heroin.

My job was to host two parties a month. All I had to do was hire a plane to take London's top DJs out there and spread the word. In return they would put me up in a beautiful villa in the hills. I put everything into storage because I realised that Smallwood Taylor were no longer going to pay the rent on the Fulham Broadway flat, and went to Ibiza.

Before I started at the Ku Club I went to stay with Peter Lansendorf, a German guy who was the spitting image of Jack Nicholson, right down to the sunglasses, evil grin and ponytail. Staying with Peter, I thought I'd put my past behind me. Then, one day, to my horror, Helen De Barge somehow tracked me down to his house. They let her in, thinking she was a friend of mine. She ran to me and said, 'Darling, I missed you so much. I thought this would be the perfect place to rekindle our romance.' I was so taken aback I nearly fell into the pool. I gathered my thoughts and said, 'Get the fuck out of here and leave me alone. I've told you it's over.' She left, but later returned and somehow persuaded Peter to let her stay in the guest-house. When I found out I was completely horrified. I had to get out of there. I rang a friend, the Dutch TV presenter Patti Brad, who was married to one of the sons of the Agnelli family, who run the Fiat empire. Within an hour she had come round to pick me up and I stayed at her place, out of Helen's reach, until the Ku Club was able to fix me up with a villa and I started to arrange their parties.

For the first party I contacted my old friend Gabriella Palmona of the Take Two model agency. She put the word around the club scene that there would be this fabulous party at the Ku, and it wasn't long before the plane was fully booked with London clubbers. Then I contacted Lee Barrett. He was now managing a band called Midnight, who were fronted by Gavin Rossdale, who went on to form the grunge band Bush. We took Midnight out there and called the party No Sleep Til London. I also took designers over there and choreographed a whole fashion spectacular. The evening ended with 5000 kids dancing to the big DJ of the time, Fat Tony. The Ku was unlike any club you'd see in London. It had a tropical theme, and had trees and a swimming pool inside.

I always liked to keep busy, and this work gave me the way to get over my heroin addiction. I started taking the heroin substitute methadone, which is a lot harder to come off than heroin itself. It takes a lot longer but at least there is no cold turkey. But one day I stopped the methadone and cold turkey started. I had cramps, hot sweats, I was violently sick. Luckily a private doctor sorted me out with some more methadone.

There were plenty of other narcotic temptations on the island. One night, I took an acid tab at rival club Amnesia, and was swinging over the dance-floor. The next day someone told me that I would not get off the swing because I thought I owned the club. At closing time I apparently broke a branch off a palm tree and started sweeping everybody out of the door. I was embarrassed, but at least I wasn't on heroin. I was getting stronger and stronger, and the club was a financial success too. The Ku Club invited me back the following year.

One of my funniest memories of the time was looking out of a balcony window one lunchtime to see the people who had been out the night before all laid out on the ground fast asleep. Fat Tony was there in his rolled up leather trousers and trainers, his legs burning in the sun. He and about 20 other people had gone to sleep in the shade, but the sun had changed direction and they were all scorched, and looked like basted turkeys.

After I had only been in Ibiza for a short while, I had to come back to England for Rusty's wedding to a girl called Miranda, who had worked at the clubs as well. Rusty set a wedding date of 12 July 1986. The ceremony was going to be quite a grand affair at Lincoln Cathedral, because her father was the sub-dean there.

About 30 of us set off on the evening before the wedding because it was an early ceremony. Halfway up on the train, however, I realised I had left my medication back in London. Sheer panic came over me. I didn't want to be going through cold turkey on the most important day in Rusty's life, in the middle of Lincoln Cathedral. The only thing I could think of was to get back to London as quickly as possible. We had just gone past a train station, so I decided to pull the emergency cord. As the train screeched to a halt, I leapt off and ran for it across some fields. The others thought that would be the last they would see of me. When the guard came down the train to find out what had happened, they just pretended that a drunk had been on the train, had pulled the cord by mistake and then run off.

I got to a small station in the middle of nowhere and waited for the next train to London. I got back, headed straight for Rosemary's flat, picked up my methadone and headed for the station again. By now though, the last passenger train had left for the north of England. I wandered around and then I had a stroke of luck. There was a milk train going up overnight. I squeezed on, and eventually, after a very expensive cab journey, got to the hotel in the nick of time. Nobody could believe I had made it, but after a quick shower we all headed off to the cathedral. Bob, who conducted the service, seemed almost as out of it as me. He called Rusty 'Randy' by mistake. I was glad when it was all over and we could all go back to the hotel for a very drunken reception. After that escapade I felt I deserved a drink.

Rusty and Miranda were a colourful couple to say the least. Before they had married, she had been a dancer in one of Arlene Phillips' Hot Gossip troupes. She later went on to be a successful choreographer herself, working with the likes of The Pet Shop Boys. It had been a bit of a whirlwind romance and soon after their wedding, when they both came out to the Ku Club, they were already arguing. One night, just before our big party when everybody was due to fly in from London, another club host was trying to get everybody to stay up and take ecstasy. I said to Miranda, 'Please don't, you've got to be up early in the morning and have a clear head. You've got a lot of work to do, you've got to be professional. Let's go back to the villa.' She agreed to come back and I went to find Rusty, who was driving. Rusty didn't need to take drugs, he was always hyperactive anyway. When we went to find Miranda to drive home, she had suddenly decided not to go back. 'Why are you so boring?' she smiled. I suspected by her change of mood and the grin on her face that she had taken some ecstasy. I had no time to mess about with her. I had a long day ahead of me and I had to make the day go with a bang. I set off home with Rusty where there was a boy from the Ku staff cleaning up, who didn't speak any English. He always thought we were a bit crazy anyway, but this time his suspicions were confirmed.

Suddenly, Miranda walked into the villa in a rage. I suspected that the calming effects of the drugs had worn off. 'How dare you leave me at the club? The taxi didn't have a clue where the villa was, and I had to walk half a mile in my stilettos to get here.' Meanwhile I had been trying to console Rusty, who was upset about Miranda's behaviour. I was having to cheer him up and calm her down and generally play peacemaker, so I thought the best thing to do was to go into the kitchen and make coffee for everyone. As I came back, Miranda was waving her hands about. She hit the cup, knocked it out of my hands and sent Brazil's finest all over the white walls of the finca. I'd had enough by then, so I said, 'Look, you two sort yourselves out. I'm off to bed.' But I couldn't get to sleep. I could still hear them arguing in the next room half an hour later. I stormed in and said, 'If you can't keep the noise down, you'll have to go and stay in a hotel.' They were quiet for a while, then gradually the noise began to build up again, except this time it was coming from outside by the pool. And yes, sure enough, suddenly there was a big splash. Somebody had been pushed into the pool. I looked out of my window and there was Rusty, fully clothed. He is not a very good swimmer at the best of times and I could see him struggling to the side and climbing out as Miranda said, 'You deserved that.'

By now it was six o'clock in the morning. I decided that I had had enough. We were due to start work at 9am. Miranda seemed to think everything was my fault so I said, 'Look, I've had enough of you, even if you are Rusty's wife.' I went into the bedroom, packed her case, threw her into the back of the pick-up truck and threw her bag in after her.

Because I couldn't drive, I had to get the boy from the Ku staff to drive the truck, and we set off to the sound of her thumping on the back each time we went over a bump in the road. Every time she screamed I just turned the music up louder. When we got to the airport, the truck stopped with a screech, I threw her luggage out, threw her out and said, 'Right, you're on the next plane back to England. Don't come back to the villa.'

By the time I got back to the villa, Rusty was all morose. He was wondering if he had made the right decision to marry Miranda – was she too crazy for him? I was busy reassuring him and telling him that I'd support him whatever he decided, when the door burst open and it was Miranda again. 'I heard every word you said, Strangey, you keep your nose out of it. I've got the police with me.' I suspected she was lying and started humouring her, saying, 'Come on, Rusty, we're gonna go down to the cells.' She was furious that I had rumbled her, and started ranting and raving. Then she walked outside, picked up a boulder and threw it at the windscreen of the truck, shattering it. I'd had enough. I decided to leave them to it. I crawled into my bed and tried to snatch some much overdue sleep.

In the morning, which was only a couple of hours later, I walked into the lounge and there, on the table, was a letter addressed to me from Miranda. It said, 'Sorry for noise last night, Steve. We've taken the car to the beach and we'll get the window repaired on the way back.' I was completely gobsmacked.

While out in Ibiza, I tried to keep my pop career going. Roger Taylor had a house out there with a studio in it and he helped me to record a track I'd written called Manipulator. We did the recording after a night of partying at the Ku Club, and it went really well. When we were next back in London, Patti Brad came to the studios to do backing vocals, and Freddie Mercury joined in too. I'd met him before, but I'd never really got to know him. He was cracking jokes and was great fun, although he was off his trolley on something. Roger loved the track so much he ended up including it on the album by his own band The Cross.

Freddie was great. I can remember going to Wembley Stadium after he died, for the Freddie Mercury tribute concert, and sitting behind Elizabeth Taylor. She was someone I'd always wanted to meet, so I tapped her on the shoulder and told her I was Welsh, and we immediately had a rapport. It probably helped that Richard Burton grew up about five miles from my house in Porthcawl.

Following the success of Ibiza, I decided that I wasn't going to go back to London. Peter Lansendorf's brother had a clothes shop in Berlin and when the season at the Ku finished, I discovered the brilliant Berlin Zoo Club and stayed there for two months. We used to drive all the way there in his bright yellow Rolls Royce with a white leather interior. It was a great way to chill out, a way to escape from the madness of Ibiza. At first there was the temptation to go to the gypsy quarter and get heroin, but by this time the demons had slowly started to leave. Club culture, which had started out in a tiny room in Soho, had gone global. I was then offered a similar job to the Ku in Italy. I went there for four months, taking plane loads of clubbers and DJs over there and introducing the Italians to the great British way of clubbing.

Life was one long party rollercoaster, a bumpy ride with incredible highs and incredible lows. Around the time that I was running parties in Ibiza, some club-runner friends, Robert Pereno and Little James, started to do a similar thing at a ski resort over the Italian border from St Moritz. They called it The White Lines tour, partly because of the snow, but mainly because of the other kind of white powder that was flying around. A plane load of about 60 people, usually wealthy men, débutantes and models, would arrive and be given chalets. My friend Mark Armstrong's brother Paul was always there. They were from a wealthy Italian family, which was linked to the Fila empire. I decided that although this holiday was great fun it did take it out of you. It was a duty-free resort, so there was drinking from the moment you got up. I sometimes wondered why I was there. I hated skiing. Miranda remembers how she once caught me rolling around in the snow round the back of the chalets so that it would look as if I had been out on the slopes all day. In reality, I started the *après-ski* when everyone else went off to ski. After the day's drinking, we would head to one of the clubs. There were some fantastic venues around there. There was one nightclub that you entered on a slide. As night fell, the girls treated the place like an Alpine King's Road, wandering around in the snow in skin-tight rubber dresses, even though it was freezing cold. The locals would look at us as if we were complete lunatics. There were some strange goings-on – which all ended up in the tabloids when it turned out there had been a reporter following us around. Luckily for me, I had left the resort by the time the story broke of right honourables behaving badly, food fights, drunk and disorderly antics, and sex in the toilets on the plane home. The partying had taken its toll and I had taken up the offer of a break at Paul Armstrong's family place in Italy, near Milan. Paul's mother, Emilia, could not have been more friendly. I got on so well with the family that when I returned to London from Ibiza I would often stay at Mark's house.

During this time I was flitting around London, but Mark and I became very close. I was frivolous with money and he helped me out a lot. Years later, in the early nineties, we would laugh about not having any money. Sometimes, for a joke, Mark and I would go out with nothing and have a competition to see who could come back with more money. We would go out, get off our faces and say to people, 'Oh god, I've got no money for a taxi. Can I borrow a fiver?' and when we got back we would see who was the winner. It was ironic because Mark, who for a while went out with Sadie Frost, was very rich. He was definitely never short of a fiver.

During my spells in Ibiza I would come back to London, either on business, or to see friends. Sometimes I would stay with Rosemary, sometimes I would stay with Mark Armstrong in Cadogan Place in Chelsea. In retrospect, it was foolish to come back. The reason I went was to make myself stronger, and I was defeating the object by coming back and getting sucked into my old ways. If I came back before I was completely clean, it didn't take much for me to relapse.

But I was always secretive about my heroin addiction. If I was with other addicts I might smoke heroin openly, but when I was with people I cared about, the last thing I wanted them to know was that I was a junkie. I stayed with Mark many times and he never knew about it. I never took heroin in front of my real friends. I never pulled out the foil and did it in front of them. I would disappear to the bathroom or toilet. In some ways I was embarrassed, and I would lie about the fact even though I had owned up in the media. Once, I was moving house and Tanya was driving the van. I was so desperate that I hid in the back behind a sofa and smoked some heroin. Tanya had no idea what was going on, but I remember her saying, 'What's that smell?' It was a deep, smoky smell, completely different from tobacco. After that she always recognised the smell.

Over the years I got very good at hiding my habit. I'd never got myself into a state where I was dirty and shabby, and my places were always spotless.

Rosemary was a tower of strength. We went off to Tunisia when I was trying to clean up and she was in charge of my medication. Methadone had a strange effect on me, particularly if I was drinking as well. We often freaked out waiters, who thought we were an odd couple anyway, behaving as if we had just escaped from an asylum. They absolutely hated coming to do room service, so to cheer up their day I used to put on Rose's high heels and her maroon dressing gown/nightie thing and be sprawled on the bed when they came in. For an added touch I would put some of her lipstick on too, and get Rose to hide behind the curtain in the back room. The waiters would always come on to me and then just as they got on to the bed, Rose would spring out from behind the curtain and yell, 'What are you doing with my husband?' They would run, screaming from the room.

It was always an adventure going away with Rosemary. In the autumn of 1987 I sold my story to Rick Sky of the *Sun* and was paid handsomely. With the nice little fee I received, I decided to escape from the winter weather and treat my friends to a holiday. I was going to go with Linda Gallagher and Rosemary, but at the last minute Linda couldn't come, so just the two of us headed off to Thailand. Now, as I've said before, I'm pretty broadminded and not easily shocked, but that holiday was a real eye-opener.

We were planning to head for the beaches, but first we had two days in Bangkok. No sooner had we left our hotel in the centre of the city, than a guy comes out of a doorway with a card telling us about all the things the women at his club could do with their vaginas. The list was endless. They could remove razor blades, open coke bottles and fire ping pong balls at you with incredible accuracy. It also said something about go-go boys, which sounded interesting, so we went up some stairs and were ushered to a table and given a drink. The boys at the bar had numbers on their wrists, and if you liked the look of one of them you could tell your waiter and they would send them over. It was mind-blowing. You are sat, having a civilised drink, and lo and behold the show starts. The room itself was mirrored from top to bottom, so everywhere you looked you could see reflections of yourself. And cocks and balls going in every orifice from every angle possible. On the table next to us was an old English couple taking it all in. They called a number over, who joined them and then they left. I suppose it made a change from bingo. Later we took a plane to Pataya, where we saw some exotic lady-boys, who were stunning, and I had a punch up with a monkey dressed in a suit. I was walking down the street when this monkey jumped on my shoulder. I wanted to strangle the bloody thing. It spat at me and then tried to punch me in the face. Rose had her picture taken with a ten-foot boa constrictor.

We rented a beautiful bungalow on the seafront in Phuket and just chilled out. We were spoilt rotten, with lobsters, crabs and fresh fruit delivered to us whenever we wanted it. You could have a massage or a manicure while lying on the beach.

When it got too hot I took Rosemary out on a jet ski and did my best James Bond impersonation, with Rosemary as Miss Moneypenny clinging on for dear life. Every time Rose asked me to slow down I went faster and jumped the waves, and I laughed as her face went greener and greener. But the next day she had the last laugh. The current was much stronger, and the man hiring out the jet skis asked me if I was experienced. I said, 'Of course', although until the previous day the nearest I'd come to jet skiing was paddling around off the north Wales coast with my dad when he was trying to chat up the women and I had to pretend I was his younger brother so that I didn't cramp his style. Of course, the bloody thing conked out. These days, safety regulations are much tighter, and tourists aren't even allowed out on jet skis on their own because there have been so many accidents. Rosemary was on the beach, but she is short-sighted and didn't have her contact lenses in, so couldn't see me waving for help. I was getting more and more worried about getting back, but I kept thinking that if the jet ski wasn't returned I would have to pay for it. In the end I was lucky. Just before I was carried out into the Indian Ocean, another jetskiier saw me in distress and towed me in. I could have stayed there for months.

On the way back, we stopped off in Bangkok for a quick shopping spree. You could get perfect copies of the latest Yamomoto and Comme des Garçons collections for a fraction of the price. The next day there was a knock on the door of our hotel room, and the shop owner started demanding that a pair of shoes were returned to him. I didn't know what he was talking about, and after a lot of shouting the police turned up. By complete accident I had taken a pair of shoes from a shop without paying. I paid up and they went away without pressing charges. It could only happen to Steve Strange.

I went back to the Ku Club for one last season as the acid house scene was beginning to take hold. DJs such as Danny Rampling and Paul Oakenfold were doing really well and were attracting a new generation of clubbers. Places like San Antonio had been taken over by people who made me embarrassed to be British. They were pissed from morning to night, and shouted, 'Where's my Heineken? Where's my burger and chips?' They had no respect for the Spanish people.

Overall, Ibiza was a positive experience, but there were some unhappy aspects to it too. When I went, I put a lot of my old outfits, such as the Melissa Caplin outfit I wore in the Fade to Grey video, in storage. I thought I would only be away for a couple of months, but by the time I came back, a few years later, the compound interest on the storage fees had mounted up and I couldn't afford to buy my own things back. The storage company told me that things get auctioned off if their owner doesn't pay the interest. Someone somewhere must have my Edwardian child's outfit and most of the costumes from Visage's videos in the back of their wardrobe.

Finally it seemed time for me to settle back in the UK. Once I hit London, I stayed with Rusty again. He had finally realised what Jean-Phillipe was like. Rusty had invested a lot of money in Trident Studios and was on the verge of bankruptcy. After a decade of fame and fortune, both of us were virtually back to square one. The only thing that had changed was the venue. Rusty was now running a club off Berkeley Square in Mayfair, and to pick up some quick money I did the door for him.

I always had an entrepreneurial streak, however, and I wanted to work for myself again. I never thought in a million years, though, that I would end up as a sticker boy, putting up advertisements for prostitutes in phone boxes. Other pop stars, names that I dare not mention, had done it in their time, so I was in good company, but it was a long way from the lavish lifestyle I had become accustomed to in Ibiza and Italy. Then, one day, out of the blue, I got a call from Ronnie, a high-class prostitute I had known since the punk days of Louise's, when she used to hang about in the club between jobs. Ronnie worked under the name of Cat Woman. She was a lesbian who hated men because of the perversions they made her do when she was turning tricks. She said she had heard that I was down on my luck and asked if I was interested in earning some quick cash. I'd get £50 a day for putting up her cards in phone boxes in the west London area. It was an unexpected offer, but there was something about the seediness of it which fascinated me, so I said yes.

I had to go to her flat in the morning, pick up 2000 phone box cards and work out my own distribution route. I'd start at Earl's Court, work my way up to Gloucester Road, then to south Kensington, the Victoria and Albert Museum, then High Street, Kensington. Doing all the phone boxes took about four hours. I soon realised it was silly taking cards for just one prostitute for all that work. I ended up doing five a day, so I was soon raking in £250 a day. You had to work hard for your money though. It was a seven-days-a-week occupation. If their phones weren't ringing, they would claim you weren't doing your job, when, in fact, it was probably the BT cleaners going round after you, taking the cards down as fast as you could put them up, or the police stopping you from doing your job. Other card boys would put the word out if they saw the police coming but, as soon as the coast was clear, you'd be at it again.

When I got back to Cat Woman's flat after the first day's work, she answered the door in her full PVC outfit complete with mask and said, 'You couldn't have come at a worse time.' The basement was full of punters. I could see a guy bound and gagged on a crucifix in the back room. She told me to sit in the toilet until she was free. While I waited, I could hear her next door in the bathroom. She was pushing a punter under the water with her six-inch stiletto heel, while he was masturbating and she was shouting, 'Drown, you dirty little fucker.' She didn't like black customers and would ask her maid to send them away because she said they took too long to come.

One day I got a call from Ronnie asking me if I wanted to earn a quick £50. She said, 'I've got a trannie here. Can you come over like a brickie in Timberlands and jeans, and make out you find her sexy?' I walked in and said, 'Awright dahling!' Standing there was a 22-stone, bearded truck driver in a Shirley Temple wig. 'What a fucking gorgeous pair of tits you've got on you. I'm having a job to keep this stiffy down. All I can think about is bending you over that table and giving you a right good seeing to. Let's feel your tits, love ...' He acted all coy, and said, 'No, no, I'm keeping my virginity.' How I kept a straight face, I don't know. But I did it, and I got £50 for it. Believe me, there were some weird scenarios.

I didn't get to know the other girls I worked for quite so well. But they should all have been done under the Trades Descriptions Act for their cards. Tamsin, for instance, was supposed to be a 19-year-old, leggy blonde, 36–24–36. She was more like 18 stone and wouldn't be seeing her teens again. Sometimes I'd pop round and she would be in tears saying, 'Why do so many clients walk out on me?' I didn't have the heart to tell her the answer.

Jan and Sian were black and white lesbians who had a rack in their lounge. A guy would be bound and tied by his feet and arms, and then they would stretch him out. They called it the Pain Dungeon. They also had a baby room, where grown men would sit in a giant high-chair, wearing a nappy and being fed from a bottle. Sometimes I'd knock on the door and they would say I couldn't come in because they had a famous client in there. There was another prostitute whose speciality was to stand on a glass table, and piss and shit on it while her clients were laying underneath. I guess it was a dirty job but somebody had to do it.

It might sound sordid, but doing the stickers was a quick, easy way to make money and I didn't think I was harming anyone. If anything, it helped the girls. Because they worked from home, they didn't have to have a pimp creaming off their profits. It soon came to an end though. I was carding one afternoon when I was stopped by the police. I was charged with criminal damage under my real name, so I don't think they realised I had a criminal record. I didn't think it was worth the risk of carrying on once the police knew me. But it had been a good learning experience and it gave me an insight into another world.

CHAPTER TEN
DREAMING AGAIN

It's funny how life has a habit of going round in circles. By chance, I happened to run into an old friend of mine from Wales, Jeanette Calliva. I had been thinking of going into partnership with Rosemary Turner, whom I had temporarily moved in with after a bit of time with Rusty, but then she became pregnant, so I decided to start working with Jeanette. We had been talking about doing something together and then, out of the blue, I was approached by European Leisure, the company that I worked with at The Camden Palace. They had now taken over the Hippodrome, the old Talk of the Town nighterie on the corner of Leicester Square that had been run most recently by Peter Stringfellow. They wanted to open with a splash, with lots of VIPs and publicity, and they immediately thought of me as the person who could give the club the push it needed. I said I'd do it as long as I had *carte blanche* to do things my way. They agreed and I started to think about setting up a club unlike any other club there had ever been.

It was December 1989, the end of one era and the dawning of a new one. If the eighties had been about thrusting shoulder pads and power dressing, the nineties were going to be about caring and sharing. Spiritual New Age religions were taking over from the worship of material things. I'd recently read an article about brain technology and brain gymnasiums – how you could stimulate your mind and get a natural high without the use of any drugs.

I travelled down to Brighton to do my research and visited some New Age centres. I was impressed by the concept of flotation tanks and intrigued by the theories about the healing power of crystals.

Everything suddenly seemed to fall into place. The designer Rifat Ozbek's new fashion collection was called Dream and all the clothes were white. I decided to call the club Dream Age and deck out the Hippodrome entirely in white. There had never been a nightclub like Dream Age. The venue was filled with snow-white artificial trees with vegetables hanging from them. Fake sprouts, carrots and cabbages were all meticulously painted white by Belinda, the mother of Ben from Curiosity Killed the Cat. The cleaners loved me. On the stage, where you might have expected to see a band, there was a flotation tank. The VIP room was transformed into a brain gym, where you put on a pair of goggles, and had visual and mental stimulation. It was a futuristic scene, but it tapped into something that was in the air. It was a club both ahead of its time and of its time. The invite for the opening night was a key-ring with a crystal in a purple pouch. It was personalised, and was supposed to bring you luck if you touched it.

Of course, the concept was all a load of rubbish. But in terms of getting publicity it worked brilliantly. The day after the launch party, Dream Age appeared in every tabloid. It worked because it was new and because there was a group of celebrities there too. Roger Taylor from Queen was there with his girlfriend Debbie Lang, actress Emily Lloyd was there, Michelle Collins was there. Michelle and I became really good friends and would often go out partying and end up rambling on at each other well into the night. Simon Le Bon and Yasmin were there and George Michael turned up to support us too. Amanda de Cadenet, John Taylor, Johnny Depp and Kate Moss popped by in the early days. Even though I had been away from the club scene in England for a few years, it was nice to know that I still had the Midas touch.

One night Leigh Bowery, the most eccentric, colourful face to appear on the scene since Blitz's heyday, came down to perform. He appeared on a rope above the crowd with a tube up his bottom and peed on the audience. It was completely over the top but helped to cement the club's reputation.

Dream Age, which ran on Mondays, was a good deal for everyone. I was able to announce to the London scene that I was back with a bang, and the club got a new lease of life, becoming a paparazzo's dream by attracting names. The Hippodrome had been a fashion no-go area for years, a byword in naffness, but, like me, it was back on the A-list again.

Since I had been back from Ibiza I had not had a permanent base. I had spent some time with Rusty and some time with Mark Armstrong and then I settled in with Rosemary, who had a nice place off the King's Road in Chelsea. But once I realised I was back in London for good, I decided I needed somewhere less crowded. I had a friend called Monica who had a big house in Eltham, about eight miles south-east of central London. By coincidence this was quite close to where Boy George had grown up in Shooter's Hill. The London property market had just collapsed and Monica was having difficulty selling her house. I said that if she was having trouble paying the mortgage I'd move in and help her out.

I soon had the run of a nice, comfortable residence and it was easy to get into London. I hated driving and I thought it would be a long way by train, but it was one station to London Bridge, then all I had to do was change and get another train two stops to Charing Cross. The only problem was when I had to get home late by taxi. It was hard to get a taxi and when I finally got one to go south of the Thames I had to give the driver directions all the way.

Moving in with Monica was one of the best periods of my life. Not having my own base was hard, but she made me feel at home, as if the house was mine. I paid my share of the phone bill and paid rent. She also started to work for me. I'd put her on the door or put her in charge of the cash because I knew that I could trust her and it is hard to find someone you know you can trust in this business.

One of the funny things that happened there was that Monica was always telling the cleaner that George Michael or Prince had just been round for dinner. Then one night, Gary Webster from Minder and Michelle Collins and some other celebrities did come over. Monica had a step that she used for aerobics and she stood on it and pretended to be Cher doing a gig at Wembley Stadium. Gary and I were backing singers and Monica even laid all of her cuddly toys out as the audience. Suddenly the doorbell went and it was the actress who used to play Melissa in Neighbours. Monica opened the door and said, 'You can't come in, it's a sell-out,' and sent her away. Of course, when Monica told the cleaner about the night she laughed and thought it was just another one of Monica's stories.

I had a great time there. I felt secure and it was great not being a junkie. When I cleaned up in Ibiza it was as if my whole world had changed. When I was off heroin, I could get up in the morning and I didn't have to wait for someone to give me some stuff. There was a new taste in my mouth. I could smell things again. I had been given a new lease of life. Although I was still taking cocaine, the heroin side was gone and it felt like a whole weight had been taken off my back. I could function at meetings without thinking about my next fix.

In the house in Eltham, Monica had two Rottweilers called Oscar and Ebby. One day, Oscar died and we had a call from a pet centre about a Rottweiler that was going to be put down. He was scruffy and a bag of bones, but we knew there was a lot of love in this dog and that if we didn't take him, the poor thing would die. We popped him in the back of the car, took him home and called him Bruno. He'd been tied up in a scrap dealer's yard round the back of an old van and must have thought all humans were despicable, because it took us a long time to get him to trust us. He became such a lovable, adoring pet. I lived with Monica for five years and it was like having a little family. Martin and Shirlie, whom he married in 1988, would come all the way over from north London. Other friends would pop by. One Christmas day my mum came to stay and cooked lunch for Monica, Tanya, Martin, Shirlie, Michelle Collins, her boyfriend, and me.

I was leading a double life, though. Working in west London in the nineties, I developed a new circle of friends who were very much the wealthy Chelsea set. Jeanette and I were on good terms with David Rocksavage, who was an actor and film director but also a member of the aristocracy. His title is the Marquis of Chumleigh – his family has close ties to the Queen and owns a huge country estate. He went out with the model and singer Lisa B, and we all went down there for the weekend for her 21st birthday party. His house was even more grand than the Von Thyssen house, which is saying something. As you drove down the long drive, you saw white deer, as you walked through the house, there were paintings of his ancestors. Every bedroom had a four-poster bed and an *en suite* bathroom. Every meal was a five-course banquet.

We also got to know the millionaire playboy Robert Hanson, and Lucas White, who inherited a £150 million fortune from his father. It seemed slightly peculiar mixing with these people. I remember saying to Jeanette that she had to be careful not to end up like the court jester, the flavour of the month. At first, when I was invited to Robert's mansion in the country I wasn't sure whether to go, but I came to like him a lot. If you were down for the weekend, it was just the normal rock party circuit which went on for the whole weekend. You were made to feel welcome by the live-in staff. Although I was a valley boy I had always been brought up to show my thanks and, as I knew Robert loved his polo, I went out on the Saturday afternoon and bought him a watercolour painting of a man on a horse, playing polo, plus gifts for his staff.

Dream Age ran for a couple of months and its success spurred me on to do something of my own again. I talked to Jeanette about opening a new club. We decided to look for a venue and found a place in Earl's Court called the Double Bass that was doing no business at all. It was like going back to the beginning, when Rusty and I had found Billy's and made it into the hippest, most popular club in London. The first night was also Rosemary Turner's birthday, and because Rosemary was a face on the London scene there were plenty of names there. Davina McCall, George Michael, and Martin Fry of ABC all turned up to wish us well.

Prince fell in love with the place. The first time he arrived you'd have thought he really was fucking royalty. A huge minder arrived, got out of the limo, came into the club and asked us to move things round. 'Can we dim the lights and can that table be moved?' 'Fuck off! We have a lot of stars in and none of them go through this charade. It is staying the way it is.' Then, one night, Prince came and invited me to sit at his table. He was tiny, tiny, tiny. I thought Michael Jackson was weird, but this was ridiculous. I didn't get a word of conversation out of him. All he did was suck his lollipop. I know how eccentric some pop stars have to be to keep up a façade, but this was ridiculous. I didn't need it, so I got up and left. He took the whole charade of being a weird pop icon too far. He was out in cuckoo-land. I had nothing on him.

Monica used to adore Prince, and he used to come down to the club quite a lot because he had the hots for Lisa B . One night, after he had been to the club, he was going off to his private party at Bagleys, a vast warehouse round the back of King's Cross station. Monica started to sulk because she heard that Prince had not invited her. Just as he was leaving Double Bass, I said to Monica, 'Don't worry, we'll definitely get you there.' I made sure we followed Prince's car as it left Earl's Court and was determined to keep it in our sights. Monica was driving as fast as she could, while I sat in the back shouting directions. We raced through red lights, screeched around corners, sticking to the car bumper to bumper. I said to Monica, 'If we lose Prince's car, you won't get into the party and it will be your fucking fault.' When we got there, we stayed right behind Prince's car and as he drove under the raised barrier, we hurtled through just before it came down. We parked in the VIP car park and caught Prince up, pretending to be with him. We didn't have any invites, but I've always believed that the secret of getting into clubs is confidence – if you behave as if you should be there, they will believe you should be there too. As we got out of the car, I said to Monica, 'Head high, girl, head high,' and we confidently marched in behind Prince without being asked for our invitations.

Whenever we finished at Double Bass and shut up shop, we would head for another club, such as Tramp. One night, we all went down with a huge entourage. Sylvester Stallone's ex, Brigitte Neilsen, joined us, as did John 'Jellybean' Benitez, who had produced Madonna's first records. Monica was also with us. When we got to Tramp we were given a prime table and ordered the club's speciality dish, bangers and mash. The upper class British super rich seem to like nothing more than eating the kind of food they used to eat as school dinners at their boarding school.

While we were eating, we were joined by Lady 'Bubbles' Rothermere. She was a colourful nightlife figure who had been on the scene since the war and had got her nickname because of her fondness for champagne. She had now taken a shine to Monica, and on this occasion, leaned over and asked Monica if she could have a bite of her sausage. Monica obliged, only to see Bubbles pick the whole thing up and down it in one in a rather suggestive fashion.

Double Bass was brilliant. It attracted all the big stars whenever they were in London. We were so well connected with the pop business I considered entering the fray again myself, only this time on a management level. There was a stunningly beautiful black American singer called Jackie Jones who used to come to the club. She had a terrific singing voice and I was going to put her into the studio and get her a record deal. Somehow it just didn't work out. She had the vocal talent but not that extra something to follow through. If the right person came along I still felt I could make them into a huge star.

The club took off pretty quickly. Celebrities liked to come down because it was an intimate, after-hours place to have a drink, and punters liked to come down because the celebrities were there. I was soon building up my little empire again. Monica did the door, I had six bar staff, three different DJs a night. In fact we were so successful, we had to open two nights a week.

Diana Ross was another visitor who fell in love with the place. I can remember her dancing on top of the piano and singing along to the music. At the end of the evening, she put her arms around me, and said I had created the perfect club.

One evening, the owners asked us if we would like to do a Saturday night. I was happy to expand, but I thought that an extra night would need some extra publicity. I spoke to Jeanette and we decided to stage a fake wedding and have the 'wedding party' to open the new night. We thought it would be a bit like an Andy Warhol-style happening.

Then the press heard that I was planning to marry Jeanette and I had an even better idea. I'd been stitched up so often by the tabloids,

I thought for once I would turn the tables on them. I decided to sell them the exclusive rights and put the word out that the story of our wedding was up for sale.

The *Sun* was the highest bidder, offering us £50,000 for the exclusive wedding night story of my marriage to my childhood sweetheart from Wales. I was cautious from the start. I'd had countless dealings with the press and while they had been nice to me at first they wouldn't think twice about hurting me. I thought that if they sent their own photographer they would realise that the whole thing was a sham, so I told them that we wanted a quiet ceremony, so I wanted to use our own photographer. They thought about it for a bit, and then seemed happy with the arrangement.

The day of the wedding dawned, 7 July, and it was a decidedly star-studded occasion. Roger Taylor was going to give the bride away. Martin Kemp was my best man. His wife, Shirlie, and Pepsi, who had been in Wham! with Shirlie, were maids of honour, along with bridesmaids Emily Lloyd, Debbie Lang and the supermodel Charlotte Weston. Keith Allen was going to play the priest but he couldn't make it, which, in retrospect, was quite lucky because if the press had seen pictures of Keith Allen in a dog collar they might have suspected that something was up.

We all knew it was a joke, but we set it up to look like a real wedding and kept up the pretence throughout. Jeanette even had a beautiful dress made for the occasion by Monica Chong, and my suit was made by Nikos. Roger lent us his white Rolls Royce and had it tied with white ribbons. We stood outside St Mary's Church in Kensington throwing confetti around. Little did the media know that nothing had gone on inside the church. We had managed to keep the paparazzi away, so that we could stick to our deal of selling the *Sun* our exclusive story. They were so desperate, we sold them an extra picture for another £1000. It felt brilliant that for once I had got the better of the British press.

After the photo shoot, there was a lavish reception back at Jeanette's house in the New King's Road. Butlers wandered round offering guests a choice of champagne or lines of cocaine, but the *pièce de résistance* was the wedding cake itself. The bottom layer of the cake contained marijuana, the middle layer contained ecstasy, the top layer contained magic mushrooms. The party went on until the club opened for other guests to join in and make it into the opening night party for Saturday's Double Bass. The irony is that by the time the club opened, a lot of the original wedding guests were so off their faces, they couldn't make it!

It looked as if we had pulled it off. But somebody had tipped off Piers Morgan, the show-business editor of the *Sun*. The next day, Jeanette and I had to be interviewed by Rick Sky. He wanted to know all the intimate details about our wedding night. Jeanette had to say I was a fantastic lover, and how we had fallen passionately in love in the office, after knowing each other for years. I said that I hadn't slept a wink all night because Jeanette had been all over me. We should both have won an Oscar for our performance. We were completely wrecked, having partied all night, but we thought we had fooled him.

Then there was an anxious moment. Piers Morgan tried to contact us to confirm the story. We avoided his calls, getting friends to tell him we were on our honeymoon, which seemed reasonable. But he kept ringing. Eventually he left a message saying that he thought it was a hoax and needed to see the marriage certificate.

Luckily, I knew someone in the East End who could help me out. Shifty was very good at forgery. He knocked up a certificate and I got someone to ring Piers to tell him that the original certificate was too precious to send but I would fax a copy over to him. That way, I thought he wouldn't be able to spot anything about it that might suggest it was not real. Unfortunately, there was a tiny error on the certificate, and Morgan noticed it. 'Rites' had been spelt 'rights'. This aroused their suspicions, and they checked the name of the registrar we had given. There was no registrar in the Borough of Kensington & Chelsea called Mrs Pearce. Piers Morgan rang up again and this time I answered the phone myself. He was furious that he had been duped. He bellowed down the line that he and Rick Sky could have lost their jobs over it. I thought it was a cheek, when it was he who had chased me for the story in the first place. No one forced him to do the deal.

In the end, we were paid a fraction of the original amount, but Morgan was not finished with me. On the phone, he warned that I should be sure to look at the next day's paper, because the shit was really going to hit the fan. I suspected that he was up to something, because he had to come up with a good story to wriggle out of trouble with his bosses. That night, George Michael came over with an early edition of the next day's *Sun*. 'Well done, Steve, you've made the front page.' He teased me, and wouldn't let me see the paper, then he handed it over. The *Sun* made out that I had hoaxed my friends for a large sum of money, that none of my friends had known it was a lie and that they had all disowned me. The truth, of course, was that they had been in on it all along, but the *Sun* had given their scoop such a big build-up, about how 'pop weirdo finds true love', that they had to do something to cover up for their mistake.

Even though I knew it was not true and so did the people involved, I felt cut up and I went underground. I'd always felt today's newspapers were tomorrow's fish and chips papers. Nonsense had been written about me before, but for the first time, the papers had really hurt me. I did feel that they had got the better of me and I was disgusted by their antics. In the eyes of the public, they had made me look like a real money-grabbing bastard, which is the last thing I was. I was worried that my family back in Wales would believe what they read, because I hadn't been able to warn them about the story. Luckily, my nan, who was 89, didn't quite realise what was going on. She saw my faked wedding picture and told my mum that I must be filming a new movie. Nevertheless I didn't want to go out. I didn't want to see anybody.

My friends stood by me. Martin and Roger came round to my house and persuaded me to go to a film première with them to show the world that we were still mates, to say to the press, 'Up yours, this guy is a great guy. We haven't disowned him.' That made me feel a hundred times better and now I can laugh about it. Maybe I hadn't made the money, but in a small way I did feel I had turned the tables on the media after all. And it didn't do the club's publicity drive any harm either.

Double Bass ran for about two glorious years. During that time it was twice chosen as the Club of the Year by the *Evening Standard*. I had a lower profile than a decade earlier but I felt just as successful. I'd achieved exactly what I had set out to achieve – to create a place that was at the very heart of London's clubland. There was something symbolic about the fact that Double Bass started out on Tuesdays – the same night we had started out at Billy's over a decade earlier.

After a couple of years of success at Double Bass, the same old thing happened. The owners thought that they didn't need me. My contract was running out, and they thought that they could run the club without Jeanette or me. That way they could cut their costs and make even more money. It was their mistake, but the life of a club tends to be about two years anyway, so Jeanette and I were more than happy to move on, although we were keen to stay in the same area. A lot of people who came to the club were from west London and we didn't want them to have to trek too far. Jeanette and I therefore opened up Bank not far away in Old Brompton Road. It was run by a great manager, Xavier, and the crowds soon followed us there. Over the next few years Bank was the place to be.

There were many memorable incidents there. When the actor Stephen Dorff was in town launching his Beatles movie, Backbeat, he came to Bank and afterwards we all went back to Robert Hanson's house in Cheyne Walk in Chelsea. I had some friends up from Wales with me too: my old bodyguard Jonathan, Darryl who ran designer shops in Cardiff and Merthyr Tydfil and a couple of others, but they weren't in awe of the others at all. I remember Naomi Campbell asking Robert what this riff-raff was doing in his house, but Robert had taken a real liking to my friends. I thought Naomi needed to get off her high horse – she was only a girl from Brixton herself. Robert was the most hospitable host you could imagine. The drinks flowed and it wasn't long before everyone was off their trolley.

I remember arriving at Robert's place with Stephen, and Bjork's producer Nelle Hooper. Nelle and Naomi were supposed to be seeing each other secretly but were totally engrossed in one another. Their tongues were down each other's throats, which was fine until they stood up. Naomi is about 5 feet 10 inches and Nelle must be much shorter, particularly if Naomi was wearing heels. He barely came up to her tits. Michael Hutchence was also there with girlfriend at the time, Helena Christensen.

When Robbie Williams was still managed by Nigel Martin-Smith he used to sneak out secretly and come to Bank. Later, when he had left Take That, he started hanging out with the then-Liverpool goalkeeper David James, who had become a friend of mine because his wife Tanya was from Wales. The singer Kim Mayzelle was so out of it one night she went into my office and had a pee on my chair. It was a strange time. My own pop credibility even returned when, in 1993, a remix of Fade to Grey by The Bassheads prompted renewed interest in Visage. Things seemed to have sorted themselves out. But then an old problem returned. I started to dabble with heroin again. I had been clean for six years, but somehow I'd been sucked in again. What is most depressing is that the relapse started when I was more successful as a club runner than ever before. I don't know what caused it, or whether the pressure of the job had anything to do with it. At the time there were parties back at Jeanette's house with a colourful array of stars pulling up in cabs at all hours. The cocaine would be flowing like water wherever you went, and heroin was part of the social scene. I don't know why I relapsed. Everything was going so well. Then one night in a club I just bumped into somebody who offered me some heroin, and I thought I'd try it just for old time's sake. But a one-off became two days and then, by the third day, I had my old habit back.

One thing I've learnt from my heroin addiction is that there is no such thing as recreational use. Every time I've taken heroin and thought to myself it was strictly a one-off, I have been wrong. And deep down I think I knew I was wrong at the time and I was lying to myself.

There's something about heroin that gets right into your brain and won't go away. It's strange how you can forget your friends' birthdays or where you've left something important, but you never forget where your dealers live. I was soon heading back to the same old haunts. If the old dealer had moved on, there was usually a new one to take their

left Jack Nicholson was a frequent visitor to my clubs whenever he was in London, but he never really took my sartorial advice, preferring to stick to his sober suits.

below Chessie's house in Seymour Walk with Holly Hallett and the late, great Phil Lynott.

foot Christmas 1982. A charity visit to London hospitals handing out children's toys (and having the odd drink on the way). Among those taking part were The Belle Stars, Alannah Currie from The Thompson Twins and Suggs and Chas Smash from Madness.

Strange change 1. Shooting the new look for Beat Boy.

Strange change 2. The Love Glove sessions with Yasmin Le Bon and Terry Haub.

Strange change 3. Cowboy cool in stetson and suit.

In Egypt making the promos to accompany The Anvil were hot, hard work, but great fun.

By autumn 1984,
I'd left The Camden Palace and
Midge had left Visage. I was still
a pin-up, but it was time to
reinvent myself again.

No. 1078 SEPTEMBER 1, 1984   THURSDAYS   20p   IR 33 (Inc. VA)

Jackie

HOOPS!
HERE COMES
ANOTHER JACKIE

SPECIAL STEVE
STRANGE INTERVIEW!

EURYTHMICS
AND LIMAHL
P·I·N·U·P·S

映像人間御用達。

right Just when artist Duggie Fields thought he had escaped from me by flying to Tokyo I started turning up in Japan, advertising TDK tapes.

below Even after my heyday I was still in demand as a style icon. London designers Boy revived my image to put me on their clothing label.

★ BOY LONDON

Clothes for Heroes

above Neighbours 1. *Joseph and the Amazing Technicolour Dreamcoat* meets the Strange gang. Jason Donovan joined by (from left to right) my good friend Monica, my grandmother, my mum and (front) Tanya.

right Neighbours 2. Kylie Minogue and I share a birthday – both Geminis, but different years, of course – and we often get together to celebrate. This was at a memorable party at Kensington Park Gardens, where the cake was in the shape of a guitar.

top If there was one person who could possibly claim to know how to have a wilder party than me it was Freddie Mercury. He was always great fun to be with — completely over the top and proud of it.

above Siouxsie, Budgie, Steve Severin and I had been friends since the early punk days, hanging out at Louise's. More than a decade later, I was still out on the town, although this was a rarer foray for The Banshees. This occasion was the opening night of the live version of *A Clockwork Orange*, starring Phil Daniels. I'll always remember an eighties night in with Siouxsie, which culminated in an embarrassing early morning confrontation with our record company Polydor.

STARS DUPED

Weirdo fakes wedding

SUN 11 JUL 90

Sun exclusive

By PIERS MORGAN and RICK SKY

WEIRDO Steve Strange conned top showbiz names into attending his FAKE wedding — so he could make £5,000, it was revealed last night.

Rock stars including Paul Young, Roger Taylor and Martin Kemp and actress Emily Lloyd were duped into believing the marriage **HAD** just taken place.

They posed for pictures outside a church with wacky pop singer and nightclub host Strange and "bride" Jeanette Calliva, 26.

Strange, 30, even produced a marriage certificate — but it was phoney. There was **NO** wedding and the stars had **NO** idea they were being set up.

PHOTOS

A Scotland Yard spokesman said last night that there could be criminal charges if the certificate was deliberately forged.

The scam was uncovered when Strange tried to sell the "wedding" photos and an interview for £5,000. He had phoned famous pals to

"Just wed" . . Strange and Jeanette, flanked by Kemp, left, and Taylor

invite them to Jeanette's house in Wandsworth, South London, last Saturday.

A close friend of Spandau Ballet star Martin Kemp said: "Martin was slightly suspicious when he arrived at the house to be told the ceremony had already taken place.

"But he believed Steve when he said he wanted a quiet service. Martin joined Roger Taylor and the others for photographs with Steve

and Jeanette in front of a near church.

"Martin is extremely upset a angry at the way he has been conn by Steve."

Strange showed The Sun the m riage certificate. But four poi prove it a fake.

WEDDING "rights" are mention when it should read "rites".

THE vicar's name is given as F

Continued on Page Seven

The *Sun* and I had a bit of a love-hate relationship over the years, which reached its peak with my Warhol-style wedding in 1990. They tried to get their own back on me for stitching them up, but my friends stood by me.

place. My public relations man Tony Brainsby, who is dead now, had a heroin problem too. I knew if I ever got stuck, he would know where a new dealer was.

Yet, while heroin dominated my waking hours, life still went on. In all the time I have been a heroin addict, I was still able to function. Unlike a lot of addicts who cling to other addicts so that they don't feel alone, I never did it socially. If I was around someone's house and I needed to smoke some heroin I would go into the bathroom where no one could see me. I would get out my cigarettes and, in the back of the packet, I would have a tube with a folded piece of aluminium and a small bag of heroin. I'd sit on the side of the bath or on the toilet, quietly unfold the foil and chase the dragon. If anyone ever had their suspicions and confronted me I would simply deny the fact that I was on it.

I say that I was still able to function, but ultimately that was all heroin enabled me to do. It enabled me to get back to my normal state, without the heroin cravings. I was spending £150 a day just to feel normal. The worst time for me was the evening. I would get into a paranoid state if I did not have my morning supply ready to get me up. However late it was, I would go to a dealer, because without that first smoke I couldn't make it to my office by 10am and I knew that dealers didn't start their day until about 12.30pm.

Why I did it, I don't know. Realising that the dabbling had turned me into a junkie again was a soul-destroying moment. How could I let it happen again? I thought of all the people I knew who had been killed by heroin. There was a girl in the Warren Street squat, two of Boy George's friends. I thought I had got rid of the demons in the back of my head, and yet they were still there, egging me on to do something which I knew was bad for me. How was I still willing to put myself through this?

My increasing dependence on drugs started to affect my working relationships. On the surface, the club seemed like another hit. It was always crowded with the same faces who had followed me from Double Bass, but behind the scenes things weren't so glittery. I was embarrassed by the fact that I was on heroin and I tried to deny it. I called people liars for making the accusations, when they were right all along. I do think the fact that heroin is illegal added to the stigma of addiction. It meant that people always associated it with criminal behaviour. At least if it was freely available a lot of the crime would stop. I suppose, in a perverse sense, the one lucky thing about my addiction was that I was always able to pay for my drugs. I am not condoning dishonesty, but I can understand why people break the law to get the money to pay for their next fix.

Heroin is all an addict can think about until they have scored. It absolutely consumes you. It's the powder power. I knew Kathy Jeung, who was in George Michael's I Want Your Sex video, when she first came to London from America. George wrote the song Monkey about her when she developed a heroin addiction. Until you've been addicted, you don't appreciate the accuracy of the description of addiction as having a monkey on your back all the time. Eventually I had to come to terms with my problem. It was about time I decided that my own house needed new curtains and I needed to stop putting new curtains into everybody else's house. The people you buy drugs off aren't your friends. Some of the dealers and situations I got into were not like anything you could imagine. Prostitution is sleazy but this is far, far sleazier. When I was buying from dealers, I'd visit their house and see other people shooting up or smoking gear on the premises. I hated that. Once I'd got my stuff, I got out of there as fast as I could.

You'd walk in and people would be sitting there with needles in every possible vein. No wonder these places were known as shooting galleries. I hated needles and the last thing I wanted to see was someone with a tourniquet around their neck injecting. It repulsed me. One dealer I knew used to inject heroin into his cock. It was the only vein he could find. I had to stand there and wait for him to shoot up before he weighed up my gram. Doing heroin was bad enough but I never went that low. Maybe a lot of it was vanity, I never wanted track marks on my arms. I'd see people with abscesses. Some people had thrombosis and eventually had to have limbs amputated.

I would always smoke heroin by chasing the dragon, heating up the heroin on a piece of tin foil. I never injected. If I had, I think maybe I wouldn't be here today. I only snorted it twice. Once was at the Paris fashion show when I thought it was cocaine. The other time was when I was at my most desperate. I bought the stuff from a dealer, and although I couldn't bear to smoke it at his house, I couldn't wait to get home either. I went into a bus shelter, chopped a line of brown powder up and snorted it.

I always feared that one day I would turn up at a dealer's and somebody would be dead from an overdose. That was another reason why I always wanted to get out as quickly as I could. Once, a girl I used to score from did overdose in front of me. I didn't know what to do. I was tempted to run, but tried my best to resuscitate her. I gave her the kiss of life and started pounding on her heart, then I put her in the recovery position. Eventually her eyes started rolling so I knew she was coming around. She didn't thank me; she didn't even know what I had done.

Waiting for a delivery was even worse than visiting the dealer. They have power over you, and they will keep you waiting for as long as they can, knowing that you are suffering until they turn up. If you phone them, they always say they are on their way and are stuck in traffic, but however long they say they will be, they always take longer. But I had to go through it, even though I could see it was taking control of my entire life. Without heroin, my day wouldn't happen. Anyone who has ever been an addict knows that it is not fashionable or hip. I'd hate to think that anyone thinks I was cool because I was a heroin addict.

My addiction also caused problems in my relationship with Jeanette, who knew I had relapsed. Everything was fine as business partners. We split everything fifty-fifty, even though people were surprised, thinking that I should have the lion's share because it was my repu-tation that made the clubs work. But I've always been generous and was happy to share everything equally.

What upset me, was hearing stories about Jeanette talking about me behind my back. She was one of the few people who realised that I was back on heroin, and while I was trying to keep my drug problem quiet, I'd hear that Jeanette had said to people, 'Isn't it sad about Steve's relapse? Isn't it a shame? I'm really worried about Steve and his heroin ...' She could have been more discreet. I knew I had a problem, it didn't help that Jeanette was suggesting, albeit sympathetically, that I was missing work because of my addiction. I was particularly sad about it because I cared for Jeanette and had always supported her. Furthermore she thought it was perfectly OK to be necking ecstasy and cocaine all night. If I had been talking about her in the same way it would have been a different story. I wouldn't have dreamt of saying anything about Jeanette behind her back. Drugs such as ecstasy and cocaine were rife in clubland, but there was always a taboo about heroin, even though it was fashionable within an élite circle of people. One of the clichés was that if anything ever went missing, it would always be the junkie who was suspected. No one ever suspected a user of ecstasy of stealing to pay for their habit, but with heroin it is the first thought that crosses your mind.

In 1994 I had a call from a business acquaintance, Fari, who said that he had just bought an old nightclub in Kingly Street, just off Regent Street, called the Studio Valbonne. Fari was very excited, 'It's an amazing place.' I was horrified. 'Fari, why didn't you call me first. Studio Valbonne is a terrible old club, it'll never work.'

He asked me to have a look first. When I went over there I was very impressed with what he had done. He had completely stripped the place of the old décor that was a tacky throwback to the seventies. What I saw instead was the potential for a brilliant new London venue. He asked me and Jeanette to come on board, and wanted to know what kind of design he should go for. I said to steer as far away from steel and gilt as possible. Go for a rustic castle feel with wooden floorboards and straw. It would be different to every other club in London and would make a huge impact. Fari took our advice and reopened the Studio Valbonne, renaming it Emporium, with Jeanette and myself managing it.

When Fari approached us to run Emporium I realised I needed a break and to come back fresh and clear headed. By staying in London the parties and the premières would be too much temptation. I toyed with the idea of going back to my roots in Wales, and David Rocksavage's offer to stay at his Sussex mansion was very tempting. In the end I decided to visit my old friend Linda Gallagher in her new home in Glasgow. As it was in December people were really in the festive spirit and there were plenty of parties, but I declined. I also visited old friends Colin and Kelly Cooper-Bar as it had been so long since I had seen them and they proudly wanted to show off their two gorgeous children, Josh and Skye.

Robert Hanson was very kind, but my heroin addiction had a destructive effect on our friendship. I heard on the grapevine that an antique vase had gone missing and because of my feelings of low self-worth I felt that I had been held responsible for its disappearance, selling it to pay for another fix. In the end, I spoke to Robert about it, and it turned out that the vase had been broken and surreptitiously hidden behind a cupboard. He had never stopped inviting me down, it was the way I felt about myself that was ruining things.

Emporium was just what I had imagined, with big gothic outside doors, ornate metal railings, wooden floor, and straw scattered around as if the building was a mediaeval ruin. It had cost Fari a lot of money, and he really wanted Jeanette and me to leave Bank, but we said we were happy there. In the end we agreed that we would stay at Bank and work at Emporium on Fridays and Saturdays. We knew we needed somebody else to come on board with us and we decided to poach Sandra from the model agency Elite Premier.

We never had a computer database back then, just a guest list of names and addresses in a file that we had built up over the years. If we were doing the Emporium on a Friday or a Saturday, on the Friday at noon we would fax every big model agency to say we would be calling to put models on the guest list. Then at 5pm I'd ring back to get the names of the models who were in town and available. I was a good friend of Sarah Dukas who founded Storm and I had known Lorraine Ashton, another big booker, from my styling days. I also had help from my old friend from Take Two, Gabrielle Palmona. We were the first club runners to do this. After a while, others latched on and copied us, so that in the end clubs all over London were filled with models. But as the first people to do it, Jeanette and I always got first pick of the best models. I knew that once we had beautiful girls in the clubs, the rich men would follow. We also had a great database of celebrities to invite to the opening night. Bank eventually lost its late-night licence and became an Irish pub and we were able to spend more time at Emporium. Xavier, our old manager from Bank, was able to join us again and the club went from strength to strength. I'd stand on the door just like the old days and Jeanette would go inside. We did an exclusive dinner party for Sylvester Stallone just before the club opened. Everything was done meticulously to please Sylvester, calling in the right wines and breads and making sure there were beautiful girls at the table.

Anyone who was anyone wanted to be seen at Emporium. Football had started to become hip again and it became the hangout of choice for the players who liked a bit of nightlife. David James and Stan Collymore would drop by when they were in London, as would Ryan Giggs. Prince Naseem and Chris Eubank celebrated boxing victories there. Lennox Lewis even came in to do some DJing.

Prince was still following me round. He chose Emporium to do his own private post-show gig. It was mayhem on the door. The street was full of Prince fans. He played his set at Wembley and then came back to our club, picked up his guitar and played the same set all over again. One night INXS had a party there to toast the release of their Greatest Hits album. I hadn't seen much of Paula Yates for a few years and by this time she had split from Bob Geldof and was living with Michael Hutchence. The party renewed our friendship.

CHAPTER ELEVEN
THE HIGHLIFE

Sometimes the past came back to haunt me in ways I could never have predicted. In the mid-nineties my old landlord Johnny Stewart contacted me. Since moving out of Kensington Park Gardens he had renovated an old mews house in Notting Hill. Johnny knew that I shared a birthday with Kylie Minogue – different years of course – and suggested I threw a party for both of us.

Turning up at Johnny's new house was a bizarre experience. Johnny had decorated it just like the old house, with antique furniture and icons all over the walls. It felt as if the old house had been moved to another place. The living room was identical, except that the furniture was in opposite corners.

The party was a huge success. The old club crowd, such as George Michael, mingled with the new club crowd, such as promoter Lawrence Malice. The old fashion/art crossover brigade was in full force, with Zandra Rhodes, Duggie Fields and Andrew Logan leading the charge. Then there was a gathering of my new clan, Lisa B and Robert Hanson, as well as Alan Keys, a seasoned stylist who now works with N'Sync, and Jason Donovan. Jason and I struck up a friendship based around cocaine. Later on we spent many evenings talking absolute rubbish well into the night at various parties.

This particular night was a spectacular event, which culminated in Kylie and myself cutting the guitar-shaped birthday cake together and getting our pictures in the papers. The last thing I can remember is falling out of a cab at home at about five or six in the morning.

There were more celebrations later on. Robert Hanson threw a party for us at his mansion in Gloucestershire. Kylie was invited to present the trophy at the polo match. It was a great weekend. Robert was always the perfect host.

Emporium lasted about 18 months and then it was time to move on. We found a place called L'Equipe Anglais, which had been owned for a long time by a middle eastern businessman known as Sharifi. We had a good team working with us. Meg Mathews hadn't married Noel Gallagher at that time and would sometimes work on the door. Most of the clubs I had run in the nineties had attracted the jet setters, who had heard that there were beautiful models at my clubs, but L'Equipe Anglais attracted the super-rich and the aristocracy. Dodi Fayed would come down. Rolf Sachs, the son of Gunther Sachs, one of the richest men in the world, would drop by whenever he was in London on business. And the It Girls were starting to crop up too. Tara Palmer-Tompkinson and Tamara Beckwith were becoming familiar faces on the scene. As usual, the rock aristocracy was there too. Kylie Minogue would pop down with Nathalie Imbruglia. George Michael was there and Robbie Williams started to make a name for himself as a party animal. It had been at Emporium that his wild side had started to emerge. On one particular occasion Robbie could hardly stand up and I had to take him to one side and say, 'Robbie, you really are a bit too out of it. People are talking about you.' He was literally falling all over the place.

But there was a delicate balance to be achieved between these guests and the public. It was tempting to give these people our undivided attention, making sure they had everything they wanted, but I didn't think that was fair. I remember one night saying to Jeanette, 'You can't just look after these people, it's the general public that are paying our wages.' Sharifi loved it when we made L'Equipe fashionable with the jet set again. He had owned the venue in the seventies when it had last been the place where the in-crowd hung out, but the original pictures on the wall were now beginning to crumble and curl up at the edges. He liked getting the new blue bloods in. It really made it look as if the club was at the epicentre of swinging London again. The only problem was that Sharifi would interfere with my guest list on the door, trying to tell me how to do my job and get his own regulars in on my nights. His had a lot of rich Arabic customers and he knew that if they came on a night when there were beautiful girls there they would spend a lot of money.

Robert Hanson had become the ultimate party host, and one day he invited me to a party he was planning in Marrakesh in Morocco, a place I hadn't been to since I had done some filming for The Anvil. It was an exclusive affair. Jeanette came too, along with Lisa B, Lisa M, Robert's then-girlfriend Normandie Keith and Colin and Kelly Cooper-Bar, friends of mine from Glasgow.

Even though everybody was a success in his or her own right, there was still an air of tension at times. When we got to the airport there was a spot of childlike playground rivalry because everybody wanted to sit as close as they could on the plane to Robert. I'd been through all of this before with Chessie, but I could sense a degree of envy when I was upgraded and given the seat intended for Naomi Campbell.

Once we reached Robert's house though, you could not have wished for a greater group of people. The house was completely over the top. Every room had its own private butler, and every bedroom door opened out on to the swimming pool.

One day we all decided to go shopping for souvenirs. A fleet of immaculate Range Rovers ferried us into the town. There was only one problem. It was in the middle of Ramadan and it was impossible to get any booze anywhere. We spent three hours hanging around, waiting for someone who had promised us something to smoke. In the end, we went away and arranged to collect the stuff the following day.

I went back into town the next day, looking forward to a relaxing afternoon by the pool, but when I returned the atmosphere had changed. Robert, who was usually such a happy-go-lucky guy, looked serious. It turned out that Jeanette, Lisa M, Normandie Keith and the other women had taken Polaroid photographs of each other, pretending they were having a lesbian orgy. Robert didn't see the funny side of it and wanted the pictures destroyed. I don't know what he objected to, I think maybe he felt that as they were staying at his house they ought to retain a modicum of decorum. I thought it was hilarious and kept one of the Polaroids. I put it in my filofax and had forgotten about it until the other day, when I opened the filofax and the picture fell out.

As evening fell, the party spirit started once again and everyone's mood lightened up. Any pretence of decency went out of the window, as the behaviour became more and more outrageous. Some of the girls were pole-dancing, others started to remove their clothes while the servants looked on. They didn't say anything, but you could tell they thought we were from another planet.

A few months after our return to London, Robert and Normandie Keith decided on a trial separation. She had started to see Lucas White, who had been on the scene since the days of Bank. Normandie was one of the most eligible women around. She was wealthy in her own right and beautiful too. I went across to New York with her and witnessed her lifestyle. Each morning, she was woken for a massage and manicure. Then, in the afternoon, she had a facial and had her hair done for two hours. She was on first-name terms with everyone at the best restaurants. She always got the table she wanted and would always have a car waiting for her in case she decided to leave at a moment's notice.

Around this time, Jeanette and I hit a bit of a sour note. We stayed at L'Equipe Anglais for some time, but as usual the owners began to think that they could run the club just as well without us. Sharifi had been OK at first, but he was interfering more on the door to get his own clientele in. Sometimes there would be arguments in front of customers, which was hugely embarrassing for all of us and definitely not good for business. We would try to avoid offending his regulars by saying that the club was closed for a private party, but more and more of Sharifi's friends were hearing that supermodels, celebrities and the general elite of the London in-crowd were going to this club, and they wanted to come too. They were big spenders, but they were spoiling the way that I'd become used to running night-clubs. Jeanette seemed happier to let them in than me, and this caused even more tension.

While we were having arguments with Sharifi about the way the club should be run, we decided on two or three occasions that we were pulling out. Right at the last minute, however, Sharifi would back down and come back to our original agreement.

In the end Sharifi messed us about once too often. At the time, I had been approached by a company that wanted to create a new central club at the Trocadero at Piccadilly Circus, so we decided to move on. They wanted to call the new club Thunder Road and I had persuaded them to change it to Thunder Drive. We went to see the place and talked to them about our ideas, but on the opening night, it did not look as we had imagined it. The most attractive aspect of the deal was that Jeanette and I got our own office, complete with our own personal assistant.

Because the owners were a large public limited company they didn't seem to care about the personal approach, which is what I'd always thought was important about a club. We got some good promoters in and had some great parties. John McEnroe and Pat Cash did a gig there with their rock band during Wimbledon. When the musical Tommy opened, starring Kim Wilde, Pete Townshend and the cast came down and celebrated with Jeanette and me. It could have been a great venue.

We were getting great press coverage, but we were finding it incredibly difficult to keep the momentum going because of problems behind the scenes. Jeanette and I were on a great wage but what people have to take into account is that we had to pay for DJs and DJ rates were going sky high. We also had to pay for flyers to be designed and printed, for people to stand outside clubs, giving out flyers, for a team of fly posters and for two people in the office. That's a lot of overheads.

People like the waiters and the bar staff were being paid a month in arrears, which meant they were virtually being held hostage in the restaurant, having to keep working in order to be paid what they were owed. And then things began to get even worse. Late payments were bad enough, but then even these became unreliable. It was no good explaining to the customers that the service was bad because of problems with pay. As the weeks went on, Jeanette and I were finding it more and more difficult and eventually we decided to pull out.

While we were twiddling our thumbs deciding what to do next, Fari tried to get us to go back to the Emporium. He had realised that without me and Jeanette on the door and doing the guest lists, the beautiful people soon stopped coming. I was tempted to go back, but Jeanette said she didn't want to. She made out that she wanted to take a break from the nightclub business for a while, but I don't think she was being very honest. She actually had plans to go into the club-running business on her own. She just couldn't bare to tell me that she didn't want to work with me any more.

It was a shame we had to stop working together, but there were too many problems between us. I still feel guilty about losing Jeanette's friendship. I had a special bond with her. We had been very close, but that had caused friction as well. When she had a daughter she asked me to be a godfather. My heroin problem was so bad I didn't feel I could be a good godfather to her child. The addiction meant I couldn't give her the love and attention she deserved.

CHAPTER TWELVE
THE LOWLIFE

After splitting up with Jeanette, I felt I needed a change of scene. I made the conscious decision now to move out of Monica's house in Eltham. I'd been there for about five years and it was time to move on. I saw an ad in Loot for a place in Bow Quarter, a new housing development in east London. When I met the letting agent Jacqui Sims, who showed me around, she recognised me and we immediately struck up a friendship. I chose a small studio flat as I didn't think I would be spending much time there.

Fari knew that I was no longer at Thunder Drive and he had asked me if I would like to work at Emporium again. I was looking round for my next move and it seemed like a good idea at the time. The club had had a big refurbishment and it was about to reopen. It was a big do, with lots of models and club faces there. At one point a man came over to me and asked me if I was Steve Strange.

Paula Yates had recently been on the front pages when a Smarties tube with opium in it had been found under her bed by her children's nanny. It was a difficult time for her because she was in the middle of the divorce from Bob Geldof and any negative coverage could jeopardise her battle for the custody of her daughters. The *News of the World* had sent a reporter to the club to investigate the story. All I said to him was, 'Can you please come away from the door, because a crowd is starting to form.' He was immediately aggressive, and said, 'I've got pictures of you and Michael and Paula doing drugs together and I've got signed affidavits.' I suppose he was hoping that I would instantly own up to something, but after a short while he realised that I wasn't taking the bait and that I wasn't frightened of him. He quickly tried a different tactic. He suggested that if I gave him the full story, there would be large amounts of money in it for me. I had one reply, 'Fuck off. Basically all you've got to do is look at Paula. She's just given birth to a healthy baby. All you've got to do is look at her birth records. That would show you she wasn't on drugs. End of story.' He put his hand in his pocket and said, 'Why don't you take my card and think about it, because there is a lot of money in it for you.' I took his card and he said that was a good idea. I replied, 'I'm not taking your card for the money, I'm taking the card so my solicitor can be on to you. You'd better do your fucking homework before you think about printing any of this because you are not going to get one guy to take the stand and say they have bought drugs off me. They might say that they did drugs with me, but that's a different matter.' I made no secret of the fact that I'd taken drugs, but I've never been a drug dealer. I don't know if this worried him at the time but his mood seemed to change, 'Now I've met you, I'm not going to use your name in the story.'

On Sunday morning at about 8.45am the phone started going. Friends were calling me up and saying I should take a look at the *News of the World* straight away. The paper was alleging that I had sold opium to Paula Yates. What was to follow was a year of hell, when my life would fall to pieces.

The security at Bow Quarter was pretty tight. It was patrolled at all times and a record was kept of who was going in and who was going out. Sometimes this level of surveillance was useful, but it was the worst thing of all at a time like this. Everyone inside those gates soon knew what was going on and I couldn't go out without feeling that everybody was looking at me. Jacqui was an angel. She came round and said if there was anything I needed, milk, food, anything, she would get it for me. I just broke down crying in her arms.

One of the problems was that this story broke towards the end of September, which in clubland is when the bookings for Christmas parties start to come in. Because our club was popular, people would book nights early before they got snapped up. Suddenly major companies were ringing up and cancelling their bookings because of the

damaging stories about me. The article in the *News of the World* made
it sound as if anyone could just go along to the Emporium and buy
drugs from Steve Strange. They made it look like I was the owner of
Emporium.

I was in a very difficult situation. I knew the story was false, but I
didn't know what I could do about it. I took independent legal advice
as I really wanted to do something. I had to take a stand over this. It
was not something I could lay down and take. In the past there had
been stories about me and I had just shrugged them off, knowing they
would soon be forgotten, but I was not going to let them get away with
it this time. Fari was away when the story broke. The duty manager
Xavier was on my side, as was the rest of the team, Graham and Denzil,
but they didn't know what to do about it. When he got back Fari took
me aside and said, 'Look, Steve, we are one hundred per cent on your
side, but I've got to be seen to be doing something about this, so I'm
going to lay you off work.' I immediately went back to the solicitor and
explained what had happened. I felt I had to fight this; it wasn't just
invading my privacy, it was telling lies about me.

My solicitor David Price said that I had a rock solid case and that I
should pursue it in court. But he was very experienced in dealing with
tabloid newspapers and he added a note of caution. 'Be prepared,
because they really play hardball. You've got to be prepared for a strong
fight here because the kid gloves will come off.'

It was hard for me, but it was a terrible time for Paula in particular.
When the story about the drugs discovery appeared I had a call from
Stephens Innocent, Paula's solicitors, saying that Paula was on her way
back from Australia and she was in a bad way because she was afraid
she might lose custody of her children. Stephens Innocent asked me
to come to their office to meet Paula. When I got there it was pan-
demonium. The world's media seemed to be camped outside in the
street and I got taken in the back way. Two minutes later Paula arrived.
She was a quivering wreck and I held her in my arms like a baby for
what must have been about ten minutes. She was saying, 'I can't believe
this. Steve, you are going to take them to court. You mustn't let them
get away with it.' I said, 'I'm fighting it, Paula. I'll stick by you.' I

consoled her, reassuring her as best as I could that she would not lose her children.

Just to reassure myself I thought about getting a second opinion to make sure my case was watertight. I spoke to Michelle Collins who had just won a court case and she said I should go to see her solicitor. He said that he had come to the same conclusions as my solicitor that my case was a solid one. But he also emphasised the risks I was taking in going to court. Having dealt with the tabloids before, he knew how they played the game and said that while they would not admit that they had been in the wrong, they would probably start by making me a laughable financial offer to drop the case before it came to court. He was exactly right, but I wasn't interested whatever the offer. I wanted to prove my innocence, not make money. They then made a second offer, which was equally laughable. Then when they made a third offer, Michelle Collins' solicitor said I should accept it, and eventually my solicitor agreed.

Taking legal action was not something I did lightly. I had a feeling that it would be a lengthy process. Having run the story as a big report I did not think that the *News of The World* would immediately cave in as soon as I objected to what they had printed. Taking the matter further was the kind of thing that I would only do in extreme circumstances, but to me these were definitely extreme circumstances. I was very lucky to have a superb solicitor working for me. David Price knew what he was talking about. He listened to my story, supported me throughout the case and reassured me, at the same time as being realistic. I had a hard time but I think it would have been a lot harder without David and his team. Newspapers had their job to do and in the past they had helped me to sell records and further my career, but I really wanted to fight this case. I was not a rich pop star with money to spare, or someone out to get their own back on the press for being given a hard time. I just wanted to set the record straight. Paula was a dear friend of mine with a heart of gold and I felt I needed to pursue the matter as much for her as for myself.

I was very unhappy and it started to take its toll on my nerves. The house next door to me in Bow Quarter was empty, and when I heard noises coming from it, I began to wonder if maybe the *News of the World* had moved somebody in there to spy on me in the hope of catching me in a drugs-related incident that would damage my case against them. I started to think that my phones were being tapped. Throughout all of this Jacqui helped to keep me sane.

I was invited over to Paula and Michael's house while the case dragged on. Paula and Michael decided to move to Chelsea. Paula had given birth to their first child Heavenly Hiraani Tiger Lily and I think they wanted to make a fresh start rather than bring their new child up in the house where Paula had been married to Bob.

They called me up to tell me they had moved and by coincidence it was just before I moved into a townhouse on the perimeter of the Bow Quarter with Jacqui. The first flat hadn't worked out because the trains were too noisy when I was trying to sleep, so we decided to get a place together. Jacqui, who is about 12 years older than me, is an ex-nurse, and was very caring and good to me. I've always had women in my life who have looked after me: my mum, Jacqui, Chessie, Rosemary, Jeanette, Monica, Linda. I was working back at Emporium again, not just doing Fridays and Saturdays but booking functions and fashion shows on a regular basis. And when Fari was not very forthcoming with my wages Jacqui would tide me over until payday, whenever that was. It was a really nice house. When you walked through the front door you could go straight ahead into the lounge, downstairs into the basement kitchen or upstairs into the two bedrooms, which were on top of each other. My room was at the very top.

It was a very civilised set-up. Jacqui would make my dinner. I didn't expect it to be on the table when I wanted it, but it just was. She was cooking for herself so she just decided to cook for both of us. Sometimes I would feel terribly guilty when I was late and a meal was ruined. It was a bit like a marriage, although it was never sexual. She would go off to work at 9am and wake me as she left. Our hours were almost back to front. If she came back and I was asleep she would sneak around so as not to disturb me.

The case was much more difficult than I ever expected it to be. I knew I wasn't a drug dealer but I had to prove it. This meant going back to a lot of my old heroin haunts. I had to go with the solicitor's clerk to the old addresses where I used to score in order to counteract the *News of the World*'s claim. I had to track down my old drug contacts – which was not easy. Dealers get busted and they may keep dealing but they move on. One day we went up to Chalk Farm, just north of Camden Town, about a mile from the Camden Palace. I couldn't remember the precise address of my old dealer and we had to go along the street knocking on doors asking for somebody called Anton. Not surprisingly everyone was a bit cagey. The smartly dressed solicitor's clerk could have been from the drug squad. I got to the penultimate house in the street and there was no answer. We were standing there, about to give up, when a head appeared at a window and shouted out, 'Steve, what are you doing here?' It was Anton.

When he came down, the clerk explained what we were doing. Anton immediately recognised the name of the dealer who claimed he had worked for me and had been paid huge amounts of money. Thank goodness Anton had a better memory than me. 'I know that name. That slimy cunt has just come out of prison and he owes me £180, because he ripped me off.' That was the icing on the cake.

It was all very stressful and I had a huge dilemma. I wanted to be cleared in court, but I also wanted the whole matter to be over. I rang Michael Hutchence to talk to him about it and I told him I was thinking about accepting an out-of-court settlement. I wanted to let him know that as far as I was concerned I had won the case. He said it was great news. He explained that he was just about to leave Los Angeles and was on his way to Australia, and that when he was next in England we should all go out and celebrate. He closed by asking me to look after Paula while he was away. I don't think this was because he was thinking about suicide, but I do think he was concerned about how much Paula was drinking.

I accepted the offer, but looking back I think I was wrong. I didn't get what the Americans call 'closure'. I think I should have gone to court, won the case and come out and celebrated with champagne and a press call and a photographer. Instead I accepted the money and received an apology in the paper.

I couldn't help feeling that Michael had a reason to be concerned about Paula. The pressure appeared to be taking its toll on all of us. The day I accepted the settlement I went over to see her. We were both happy that the matter was over, but there seemed to be something bothering Paula. I noticed that she was not her normal self and that her mood would swing from happy to sad at a moment's notice. She'd be laughing, then down. That night she was supposed to be taking her daughters to the filming of the ITV show *An Audience with The Spice Girls*. While she was waiting for her make-up artist to come over to her house, she got three bottles of red wine out and she seemed to finish the first one in five minutes flat. She was making all sorts of odd jokes about how I'd be happy when her make-up artist arrived because we were a perfect match.

I was in two minds about whether she should go to the concert because of the state she was in, but the girls were all excited about it and the girls were all that mattered to Paula. The make-up artist arrived and transformed Paula. She came out of the bedroom as the Paula that everybody knew and loved. This semi-drunk person had become a goddess. Her close friend Belinda came round too and said that she would go to the recording with Paula and see that everything was OK. I took Belinda aside and said that I didn't know whether Paula should go, but she said it was for the best. Belinda was very protective. But the evening turned out to be a disaster. Paula and the girls went to the recording, but Paula's behaviour was so erratic she was asked to leave.

Two days later I got a call out of the blue saying that Michael Hutchence had hung himself. I said, 'You are sick,' and put the phone down. The phone rang again and it was Monica. She said it was true. I just couldn't believe it. Then the tabloids started ringing me. Even the *News of the World*.

Everything had happened so fast it was almost too much to take in. We had won, then two days later Michael hung himself. It was devastating anyway, but even more devastating because there was no suggestion in his voice when either myself or Paula had spoken to him that he was even upset. Then two days after that Paula tried to commit suicide. But this wasn't the end of it.

I will never forget the day. It was only a couple of days after Paula's suicide attempt. I had just come in from Emporium and we were having freak weather conditions. It was pouring with rain and there were hailstones as big as golf balls. I remember saying to Jacqui that I had left my windows open upstairs. If only I'd gone up to close them. But I'd had a hard day at Emporium, and to say it had been a stressful time is an understatement. I just wanted to sit down, chat to Jacqui and have a bite to eat.

After about half an hour I said to Jacqui that I could smell burning and that someone must be having a bonfire or a barbecue. A few minutes passed and the smell seemed to be getting stronger. I thought that maybe something was smouldering somewhere. I went upstairs and the living room was fine. I went up the next flight of stairs to Jacqui's bedroom. The door was closed. I opened it a tiny bit, and a huge cloud of black smoke bellowed out. In shock, I gulped it down and started choking. I'm an asthmatic, and it didn't take much to set off an attack. Jacqui yanked me back. It was sheer panic. We stood there, frozen, then after a moment, which seemed like an age, we ran downstairs to try to phone the fire brigade, but all the phone lines were dead. The wires must have melted in the heat. We ran outside and tried to find a neighbour, but it was the middle of the day and most people were at work. Eventually we found someone and called the fire brigade who, to their credit, were there in about four minutes. But by then my bedroom was completely destroyed, Jacqui's was ruined and the water that the fire brigade had used to extinguish the blaze had ruined the lounge too.

When we went back the next day, it was soul destroying. I had lost everything. At first I couldn't take it all in. The television was gone, but that was not so bad. My clothes were gone, but even that didn't seem so important. The worst thing was the fact that my whole past had gone: my stage clothes, photographs, Visage memorabilia. The leather suit I had worn for the Anvil album cover. And then all my business things were gone too: my diaries and my phone books and my filofaxes, which were my bibles. And as each day passed I remembered more and more important things. Just one filofax survived the inferno – the one with the Marrakesh lesbian orgy picture in it. At least I could still do my job, as some of my database had been on Jacqui's computer, which had been salvaged. But that was all I had left. Forty years of cherished memories, all the ups and downs, had gone up in smoke.

There was no chance of even moving back into the house and trying to live there while it was renovated. It was gutted. The owners tried to blame me because they knew that I smoked heavily and thought I must have left a burning cigarette on the bed or something. But I told them that I had only just got in from work and had not even been up to my room to shut the windows. The investigators concluded that the fire was caused by a dodgy storage heater.

I'd won my case but I couldn't help feeling a little paranoid. It seemed to me that everything I had won was being taken back. And with Michael and Paula's tragedies there seemed to be too many awful things going on at the same time.

But there was worse news to come. Jacqui and I had only been in the house for three weeks and we soon realised that we had not had any insurance. I had lost everything. Some things were irreplaceable, but I could not even replace my clothes. All I had was what I was standing in. To add insult to injury this was when the *News of the World* decided to run their apology as agreed. But while the original story had been a major feature this was not as prominent. They had paid costs and made an out-of-court settlement, but it did not seem to be remotely enough to warrant what I had been through.

The fire was the culmination of the most traumatic period of my life. Everything I had worked for was gone. I'd fought my way back from drug addiction twice to end up like this. Ever since I had been 18 I had always had my own place and then suddenly I was like a lost soul. I had a plastic carrier bag with a few things in it and that was about it. I was lucky that at least I had supportive friends. People like Meg Mathews offered to put me up, but I couldn't hack it. The days of staying in the spare room with Rosemary or Monica were behind me. I had to get my head together.

It was the same as when I first tried to come off heroin. I had to go back to my roots to find some meaning in my life. I decided to go back to Wales to get my head together.

Back in Wales and broke I went to sign on at the dole office. The lady behind the counter recognised me as she worked out my entitlement. '£59 a week. That must be like a night out for you.' 'Yes. And the rest.'

CHAPTER THIRTEEN

BREAKDOWN

Luckily I had a house in Porthcawl that I had bought when I had a bit of money. A while earlier mum had been having problems with her boyfriend Dave and she came to me one day, very upset, saying she wanted to leave him. So I suggested that she move back to the old house in Newbridge, which she had rented out when she had moved in with him in Porthcawl. She said that she didn't want to go back to Newbridge, so I said I'd help her get a mortgage to buy somewhere. She was worried about getting one at her age, so I offered to help if Tanya would come in too. I arranged everything through friends in London, bought the house, which I also put in my mum and Tanya's name, and then a month later my mum went back to her boyfriend, which really hurt me after all the hard work. If I had sold the house, I would have lost a lot of money, so I had a crisis meeting with my sister. I suggested that Tanya moved into the house and took in lodgers to cover the mortgage. Tanya agreed, which meant I didn't have to put the house back on the market.

So I came to Porthcawl and moved in. It was weird living in my own house with virtual strangers. After all those years of living in London and having my own space it was disconcerting seeing other people in the kitchen in the morning. I had been independent since I was 18 and wasn't emotionally prepared for this. The whole process of moving in should have been a good idea. This house should have been the perfect bolt-hole from the pressures of London, but it just made things worse. At one point, one of the lodgers turned out to be a speed freak who would inject amphetamines. We had to throw him out, the last thing

I needed at a time like this was an addict under my roof. It felt claustrophobic and I couldn't get any privacy, so I had the loft converted into a bachelor pad. This meant that I had my own space, but I don't think it was good for me. I didn't have a job and couldn't settle.

I preferred Porthcawl to Newbridge. When I had gone back to Newbridge in the past, all the school kids who had never wanted to be my friend suddenly wanted to see me because I was famous. I couldn't stay for more than a couple of days without it getting on my nerves. But Porthcawl was like a new start. It was only a short drive away but there weren't the same connections.

I had gone to Wales to get over the things that had happened, but instead I was just keeping myself busy, taking my mind off it and storing it all up. I would have to deal with it at some point. For a while I did the PR for a bar in Cardiff called Scotts, but it was short lived. I got Simon and Yasmin Le Bon to come down and got some good crowds in. Jamie and Louise Redknapp and Michelle Collins were also lined up, but the same old thing happened. The manager saw the money pouring in and thought he could run an equally successful club without me and we fell out.

But not being busy was almost as bad. When I stopped working I ended up having too much time on my hands and I kept going over things in my head. I kept wishing I'd done things differently. My main obsession was that I shouldn't have settled the case, I should have gone to court. I kept turning this thought over and over in my mind, regretting what I had done, even though at the time it had seemed like the right thing. But I wasn't talking to anybody else about this. I was bottling it all up, sitting in my room, brooding over it.

I think another problem with Wales was that I was used to the culture of London, having theatres, cinemas, clubs and restaurants to go to. In Wales there was absolutely nothing for me. Porthcawl is a seaside town but I was too old for funfairs, and the clubs weren't my kind of club. I was getting even more depressed because there was no culture at my fingertips. The longer I was in Wales, the more a black cloud hung over me. When I started to get better and visited London, the more time I spent there, the less I wanted to leave and the better I felt.

One day I went out to Bridgend, about eight miles away from home, but I was still thinking about the court case. I decided to go home but I couldn't find my way back. I went to a phone box and tried to call up Tanya. But the digits were all muddled up in my head. After getting about a dozen wrong numbers I finally got through. I said I couldn't find my street. She told me to read out the address written in the phone box. When I read it out, she said, 'Don't worry, Steve, stay there, I'll come and get you.' I had thought I was back in Porthcawl, but the reason I couldn't find my house was that I was still in Bridgend.

Over the next few weeks Tanya and my mum really started to worry about me. First of all I stopped going out and then I stopped speaking to people on the phone. If somebody rang for me, I asked Tanya to say I wasn't in. If I answered the phone myself I pretended to be my brother John, even though I had never had a brother. If people came to the house I didn't want to leave my room to see them. I became like a hermit. I even stopped caring about my appearance, which was the most out of character thing of all. I was unshaven and I was losing weight. My mum called a doctor, who diagnosed acute depression and said I was on the verge of a nervous breakdown. He suggested that I go straight to the Princess of Wales Hospital in Bridgend for further treatment. I was sectioned because I was thought to be a danger to myself, but I was so disorientated I didn't even realise that I was deemed a suicide risk.

When Jacqui heard what had happened she came to Wales to see me. But through a combination of my condition and the medication they had put me on to treat it, I can't remember being in the hospital or Jacqui visiting me. Yet I was there for almost a month. After I had been discharged, Jacqui came to see me again to help me out. When she saw the condition I was in, she was appalled that they had let me leave the hospital. My weight had plummeted to seven stone. I was so depressed I had lost my appetite. It was as if I had lost the will to live. Jacqui carried me down from my room, made me bath and shave and then propped me up in the back garden and made me eat.

What shocked Jacqui the most was the amount of medication I had been put on. Every day I was taking six Prozac, four Valium, Rohypnol to make me sleep and various painkillers. I was like a zombie. My doctor would only prescribe a three-day supply at a time to minimise the risk of an overdose. Even though I was supposed to be on the road to recovery I still found it difficult to leave the house. I still couldn't speak to people on the phone. The only time I went out was to visit the doctor. I told him I was unhappy about the treatment. I felt strange, but he said once the Prozac kicked in I would be fine. It was the drugs making me do things that were completely out of character. I had shoplifted as a kid, but now I started again for no apparent reason. I suppose the oddest thing I tried to steal was an eight-berth tent. Not that I'd ever go camping. I went to my doctor and told him that I was doing things out of context. I could work out in my head why I had done it – I felt that I was homeless – but there was no real sense to it. I didn't get a kick out of stealing, I was not doing it because I needed the things I was taking.

When this happened for the first time, I explained to my doctor that I was feeling unusual, that at times I felt as if I was superhuman and could do anything, and that at other times I felt as if I was invisible. I had also walked out of Boots with a make-up kit. He thought that maybe I had been given too much medication, but despite changing my medication the problem didn't go away. My behaviour was becoming increasingly erratic. Sometimes I'd just start laughing hysterically for no apparent reason.

About two weeks later, things got even worse. Tanya, my mum and Jacqui had been fantastic and I'd always been the kind of person who, if somebody was nice to me, I wanted to be nice to them. Tanya had been really supportive and I wanted to show my appreciation. Her two lovely children, Kyle and Conor, mean the world to me. They are particularly special to the family because we all thought Tanya could never have children. Their births made her life complete. Tanya's son Kyle was approaching his birthday, so I went to Marks and Spencer and chose a jacket for Tanya. I also picked up a Teletubbies doll – Po – for Kyle. I went to pay for the toy, but there was no one on the checkout. I must have walked out of the shop, because the next thing I knew I was surrounded by security guards who called the police.

When my case came up in court, my condition was explained. It was revealed that I was currently on bail for stealing a £15 lady's coat from Marks and Spencer in Cardiff and had also taken a £25 cosmetics gift set from Boots in Bridgend. In all, I committed five offences in one day. The hearing was quickly adjourned while they waited for psychiatric reports. I talked to Jacqui about how I was feeling, and decided that for the sake of my own sanity I needed to find a group to help me sort out my problems without being pumped full of drugs. I found a group called DASH – Drugs and Alcohol Self-Help – in Bridgend.

DASH ran one-to-one counselling therapy sessions. Helen, my counsellor, helped me a lot. She talked to me and took me through every stage of my life, from my abuse as a child to my heroin addiction. There were also group meetings, when mum and Tanya came along and I found out how they had had difficulties coming to terms with the fact that I was bisexual. Where sex was concerned my mum was very old fashioned. A long, long time ago my grandfather's brother had been disowned by the family for being gay, and those values had been drummed into her head. Coming along to DASH helped my mum understand me better. She realised that fame is not as easy as it seems.

The sessions were tearful and traumatic, but things were finally coming out into the open that I had bottled up for years. It was like a huge weight off my shoulders. Slowly but surely the medication that I had been prescribed was reduced. At last, I could feel myself getting back to normal. My GP, Dr Mark Overton and his receptionist Linda Sullivan were marvellous. And DASH could not have been better. It made me realise that when you have a breakdown all your self-respect, creativity and confidence go out of the window.

And then the worst thing that could have happened, happened. The shoplifting case came to court on 6 April 2000, and it got into the papers. It takes a long time to get over a breakdown, and it had been nearly a year to the day between seeking help and the headlines. The stories made it sound as if I had only just been arrested and charged.

Even though I knew it had happened a year ago, it brought it all back to me.

I was given a three-month sentence, suspended for a year, so that I could take advantage of a probation order. My solicitor Mel Butler argued strongly against a custodial sentence, explaining my problems and saying, 'There is a substantial risk of self-harm if he is sent to prison.' I don't think I was suicidal at that point, but I did want everything to be over.

One of the worst things about it was the shame I had brought on my family, who had been so proud of me when I had been a success. One day in the high street someone said to my mum that I had been on the television the previous night. She thought it must have been one of those nostalgia shows, but in fact it was a news item about the court case. Having just got over a nervous breakdown, national publicity was the last thing I needed. I had just about rebuilt myself, but when the story appeared, it was back to square one. In fact it was even further back than that. I went down an old road, the road of temptation.

I wanted to take heroin again. South Wales had changed since the eighties and heroin had hit the valleys with a vengeance. It was rife everywhere. But it was a completely different type of drug scene. There were no jobs. No prospects. In Wales, kids seemed to be taking it out of boredom. For a month, I started to hang around the drug dealers and users in Porthcawl. This was nothing like London. These people were the lowest of the low. By comparison, the dealers in London were reliable. These people would rip you off for a tenner. Everyone was cutting everyone else's throats to pay for their own habit.

It was easy to slip into this lifestyle. Heroin has that effect on you. If you are addicted, you don't care what you have to do to get it. But I was lucky. I met someone there, Cheryl, who had two small daughters, and Judith and Melanie. Cheryl tried very hard to make me realise that I had to start looking after myself and stop lining the pockets of the dealers. Then Judith took me aside one day and said to me, 'You remind me so much of my son, and he died of a heroin overdose.' It jolted some sense into me. I think mum and Tanya realised I was slipping down that path, and I could see the hurt it was causing them. I was only back on heroin for a month, and I managed to pull myself back from the brink. But I realise now it could have gone the other way too. I'm very lucky to be alive.

The one good thing that came out of my story appearing in the press was that, after a while, I started to get letters of support. I think this also helped me to get off heroin. Johnny Vaughan was a great help when he invited me on to the Big Breakfast to talk about what had happened. On the way to the studio, I had this preconceived idea that he would take the piss out of me for the Teletubbies thing, but he couldn't have been a nicer bloke. I didn't want to do the interview inside the house, because I thought that would trivialise it and Johnny agreed, so we decided to do it in the shed which was much more sensitive and one-on-one, without the hustle and bustle going on. Afterwards, the response from the public was remarkable. People who had no idea where I lived wrote to me care of the Big Breakfast studios. Strangers wrote telling me their problems and sympathising with what I was going through. This gave me an inner strength and helped me to fight my addiction.

After my conviction, I had been put on a special probation scheme called STOP – Straight Thinking On Probation. But I don't think it was the right treatment for me. I could have learnt more about breaking and entering, stealing cars and dealing drugs there than anything else. Group meetings were no use to me at all. After about eight of the planned 16 weeks they took me out of the meetings and decided I had benefited from it as much as I would. My probation officer realised that my stealing had been a cry for help. When I tried to walk out of the shop with an eight-berth tent under my arm, I clearly wanted to be caught.

While on STOP, though, I did befriend two young boys, Ritchie from Porthcawl and Taffy from Kenfig Hill. Every Monday morning we had to meet outside the probation office and they would send us in a taxi to the STOP meetings. The meetings were very sad because quite a lot of people could barely read or write. They were so nervous that when it was their turn to talk, you could see them shaking. I felt sorry for them. After a while, the people who ran the group let it be known who I was, and that upset me because the others started to ask me questions about how much money I got every time my name was in the papers. They thought I had been paid for the stories that had appeared about me when I had been arrested for shoplifting.

It was the great British public that helped me more than probation. There was one letter in particular that helped me to start to turn everything around. The letter was from a man called Mark, who worked for Vince John Thomas and his wife Wendy who run the Moss Hill Holistic Healing Centre in north Wales. The footballer Bryan Robson had been there when he had been injured. Vince has healing hands and had helped Bryan Robson get back into the Manchester United team. The letter was forwarded from the Big Breakfast to my probation officer who suggested I went there. I remember thinking, 'What have I got to lose?' On the journey up there, I wondered what I had let myself in for. But I do know that when I left that place I had never felt so much love.

It was a big house high up in Snowdonia. The idea was that spending time there would heal my aura. Everything was geared towards purifying the body. I ate only organic food and there were sessions of massage and a type of reiki, an intense form of massage. There was meditation too. Vince uses it to purify the insides of your soul. Through meditation, you would imagine yourself on a journey. You'd then concentrate on a certain colour which would take you through past good and bad experiences and makes you feel stronger in yourself. After the breakdown, through lack of confidence, I was really under-selling myself. I didn't believe in myself. When I left, those thoughts were left behind and I was a different person. The experience was so rewarding, I didn't really want to leave. I had rediscovered my inner strength and got my confidence back again. The old Steve Strange was making a welcome return. When I got back to Porthcawl, I was ranting and raving about how fantastic this place was to anyone who would listen. I think it was fate that Mark and Vince found me, and it pushed me in a new, positive direction. Without them, I would still be stuck in Wales under a cloud of doom and gloom and possibly worse.

The next time I went, I wasn't as apprehensive, I wanted to go. In some ways, the place was like a health farm, but a far more spiritual health farm. You were pampered, but you also had to be up at 7.30 in the morning. You had a cup of tea and then you set off on a long walk. This wasn't so much for the exercise as to clear your mind of mental debris and give yourself a chance to think. It was a marvellous place. Vince even cleared up my asthma. He was a gentle giant of a man, who would put his arms around you like a bear hug and squeeze all the badness out of your body. I can't thank Vince, Wendy and Mark enough. I think I owe my life to that place.

CHAPTER FOURTEEN
BACK TO LIFE

As I began to feel healthier, both mentally and physically, I decided to stay in Wales. I love London, but when you are weak, there are too many temptations in London. I had to keep myself busy. I'd always believed that the devil finds work for idle hands. I decided I would make some use of my knowledge of the music industry and go into band management.

People asked me how come I was doing something like this, but it seemed like a natural progression to me. I knew all the pitfalls of the pop business. I still had some very useful contacts. I wanted to pass on some of my experience. At the same time, it helped me. I'd always been ambitious. I needed to have a goal to get some drive back into my life. I'd already tried to help some local kids before my breakdown, but the Non-Edible Vegetables had failed in their bid for world domination. Maybe their name had something to do with it, but maybe my emotional state at the time didn't help. I felt much stronger now.

I found another young band. They had a better name, Jeff Killed John. They could have done really well, but I had a problem with the father of one of the members, who had previously handled the band's affairs. He just couldn't accept that I was in charge.

After doing a few photo shoots, borrowing clothes from my old schooldays boss Robert Barker, the band started to take shape with an image. Then I wanted to get their name known on the London scene, so I set up some gigs. The first was at Sean McLuskey's 123 Club in the East End. The show went down really well, so I got them another gig at a swish Mayfair club. Rob Dickins, one of the most experienced record company bosses, said the drummer reminded him of a young Keith Moon. Everything seemed to be falling into place for them. Using my contacts, I got Jeff Killed John a prestigious showcase gig at China White in Mayfair. It was well received but they weren't happy because they weren't getting any wages, just petrol money. The father said that they would rather be doing gigs in Cardiff and earning £70. I had to explain to them that if they did that, they would always be doing gigs in Cardiff for £70. If they wanted to make it, they had to come to London and take a pay cut. In the end, there was too much conflict between myself and their previous manager. It didn't even come down to a 'choose him or me' situation. I'd just been around the business too long to have to put up with it. But I was annoyed and frustrated because I'd always been an innovator and I knew the band was ahead of their time, predating the fashion for high energy guitar music by two years.

I had also been thinking of working on this book. I'd turned 40 and I'd just gone through a traumatic period in my life. I'd seen close friends of mine die. In September 2000 Paula Yates died of a drug overdose. We'd lost touch when she moved to Notting Hill because I didn't have her new phone number, but I was really upset when I heard the news. We had had so many good times together, it was hard to believe she was gone. She was the world's best mother and adored her children, but I don't think she ever got over the tragedy of Michael's death. Events like this made me reassess my own ups and downs and get my priorities right. I thought it would be better for me if I left Jeff Killed John to their own devices and concentrated on my own life for a change.

I'd like to end the book by saying I'm clean, serene and ready for a new beginning. I'm certainly not about to fade to grey. I'm getting back into clubland but in a different way, maybe more in the background than on the door. I'm part of a public relations company called Ego PR, with Rosemary Turner and Dylan Watkins. I've certainly had plenty of ego myself in the past. I meditate now and I've even been to a Buddhist meeting. Maybe the answer isn't money. It certainly isn't drugs. I have reached the point in my life where it is time to change.

Although I was happy living in Wales with Tanya, her husband, Chris, my two special nephews, Kyle and Conor, and the lodgers, Les, John and Rolly, I wasn't contented. Mum lived literally five minutes' walk around the corner and after I had a heart-to-heart with her and Tanya, they realised that I was yearning to move back to London. We talked for what seemed like hours and hours. I apologised for all the hurt and agony and embarrassment I had put them through. Being clean put a whole new perspective on things. I could see on their faces that they were seeing the real me back again. We all cried, but we were crying tears of happiness. I recalled what the man in the bed next to me in the Princess of Wales Hospital had said to me, 'You've got a family that really care and love you.' They are my world and I love them dearly. Kyle and Conor in particular mean so much to me. And I was so happy for Tanya, who had finally found her diamond in Chris.

I don't know if I'll ever have my own children. I've had so much to deal with, I haven't even thought about having a relationship for five years. But when I started to sort myself out, I went to the doctor and had a thorough examination. I wanted to make a clean break from the past and had an Aids test. When the result came back negative, I breathed such a huge sigh of relief. I was given a complete clean bill of health. When I think of the way I have abused my body over the years, I cannot believe my good fortune.

Maybe I should have listened to mum when she said, 'Steven, why is it always you that pays for everyone? When things change, these people won't be around.' Some of these words are true, but I've been lucky. My real friends, like Rosemary Turner, Gabrielle Palmona, Linda Gallagher, Monica Gieruta, Liza Karamorzis, Jacqui Sims, David Rock-savage and Mark Armstrong, were there when the boat did hit rock bottom. Liza, David and Jacqui knew the trouble I was in financially and dug deep into their pockets, and I thank them dearly for helping me out. Dorian Bowen from Porthcawl was another friend whose help was invaluable. Trevor and his wife Trisha were always there in times of need. Trevor also helped me out, driving me back and forth between Wales and London when I couldn't travel any other way. I put my friends through a lot of anguish, but my real friends stood by me.

Miranda, too, was always ready at the end of the phone with a listening ear, along with Cheryl Cooper whose advice guided me back onto the right path. And then an old clubland acquaintance who was in prison contacted me after the Big Breakfast. I never judged him. One thing I've never done is to be judgemental. I think every family has a skeleton somewhere in its cupboard.

So I moved back to London and set about making a new future for myself. One that acknowledges the past and moves on from it. The funny thing is I'm clearly not alone. Only the other week I was hanging around outside St Martin's College in the Charing Cross Road. It was the place where interesting-looking people emerged in the late seventies, and they are still emerging from there today, so I was standing there looking for people who might have been suitable for a new project I was working on. Suddenly I heard a voice shout out, 'Steve!' I looked round and just about recognised my old punk chum Wendy Tyger. She was now Wendy Pearson and was working in the college administration office. It seemed like fate that we had bumped into each other in the shadow of my old stomping ground. I thought back to the time we had been dancing in Tramp and her two-piece had come undone. It felt like a million years ago. She hardly seemed like the same person. Sometimes there comes a point when you just have to put the past behind you.

Times have changed. Chris Sullivan's Wag Club had its closing down party last year. I went along and saw a lot of old familiar faces. I suppose some things never change though. Boy George and I still have a bit of a love–hate relationship. He wrote a song about me in the mid-nineties, Mr Strange, which looked back apologetically at his envy of me because I had a hit single before him. He finally admitted he had got over his bitterness, with the line, 'Forgive the hateful things I say and do.' I guess we've got some things in common though – we were both misfits when we grew up and were attracted by the bright lights of the punk scene, but that's about it. We are still friends of a kind though. He invited me to his fortieth birthday party last year. We've all changed, and I definitely prefer the George of today.

Yet as much as things change, the more they stay the same. Spandau Ballet split and went through an acrimonious court case, but I'm still friends with them. Gary is acting, Martin is doing pretty well on television and Steve, John and Tony still play together. The other night, Steve Norman called me to ask if I was coming down to their Swansea gig. Thanks for the notice, Steve! And then there's Taboo, the West End musical that tells the story of the era. The eighties seem as fashionable and relevant now as they were 20 years ago. Kids now love the music just as much as people who were kids then. The electronic music that we pioneered has become the dominant rhythm of the pop charts. Sophie Ellis Bextor's début album sounds just like an early Visage album.

Sometimes the most touching things happen. A few months ago I went out to Robert Pereno's latest West End club. It was so hot and smoky I had a rare asthma attack. Because Vince had helped my asthma so much with his bear hugs I didn't have my inhaler with me. As I started to splutter, Robert called out over the PA 'We have a VIP in the house who needs a ventolin inhaler. Does anybody have one that Steve Strange could borrow?' Suddenly a crowd of hands shot up. I didn't realise so many clubbers were asthmatic. Or that so many clubbers in 2001 knew my name. It was surprisingly moving.

A Japanese fashion company recently did a collection called Romance and they wanted to use my Fade to Grey image on their labels. The guy that arranged it gave me a present. It was a suitcase full of my old clothes that I'd not been able to pay for when I wanted to get them out of storage. He had seen them advertised in the free ads and had bought them for me. It was a nice gesture, as my past came back to haunt me.

I think having a sense of humour has helped. When I returned to clubland this year with my new night at Opium in Dean Street, I called it 'Chasing the Dragon'. Someone else was bound to make the drugs reference, so I thought I'd get it in first.

When I look back at my life, I think I've been very lucky. Lucky to have such a supportive mother who has had to put up with so much over the years. Lucky to have had such a successful career and to have fulfilled so many of my ambitions. Lucky to have lived through such exciting times. But most of all, lucky to be alive today.

Towards the end of 2001 I had a telephone call: 'I bet you think I want something don't you?' I recognised the voice immediately as Boy George and I guessed what was coming next. 'Well, you're not wrong.' George was heavily involved in putting together the eighties-set musical Taboo, and, having decided to include Fade To Grey on the soundtrack, needed some more co-operation from me. 'I think you should be involved, Steve. You are going to have a heart attack when you see the guy who is playing you, he has your voice off to a tee.' George asked me to meet my new alter ego, Drew Jaymson, to put him at his ease. I couldn't really imagine anyone impersonating me, but when I met Drew I could immediately see what George was getting at. I can just picture him, standing outside the real-life Billy's in his – or rather my – French Revolutionary garb, silver-topped cane in hand, behind the gold rope, vetting the potential clientele. Drew was as nervous about meeting me as I was about meeting him. He was slightly taken aback that I was not quite what he expected. Drew wanted to capture my personality but also capture the bitchiness of the era, when it was all about being seen wearing the right designer labels and drinking the right champagne. Here I was in 2002 telling myself how to be me 20 years after it all began.

UK DISCOGRAPHY

1978. The EMI studio sessions recorded with Midge Ure. Never released as a single. Stiff attempted to release this in 1982, but it was never officially released
A. In the Year 2525
B. The Eve of Destruction
B. All the King's Horses

1979. Single: Radar 7/9/79
A. Tar
B. Frequency 7

1980. Single: Polydor 10/11/80
A. Fade to Grey
B. The Steps

1980. Visage Album: One Way Records, Polydor 10/11/80
1. Visage
2. Blocks on Blocks
3. The Dancer
4. Tar
5. Fade to Grey
6. Malpaso Man
7. Mind of a Toy
8. Moon over Moscow
9. Visa-Age
10. The Steps

1981. Single: Polydor 2/3/81
A. Mind of a Toy
B. We Move

1981. Single: Polydor 29/6/81
A. Visage
B. Second Steps

1982. Single: Polydor 8/2/82
A. The Damned Don't Cry
B. Motivation

1982. The Anvil Album: Polydor 8/3/82
1. The Damned Don't Cry
2. The Anvil
3. Move Up
4. Night Train
5. The Horseman
6. Look What They've Done
7. Again We Love
8. Wild Life
9. Whispers

1982. Single: Polydor 18/6/82
A. Night Train
B. I'm Still Searching

1982. Single: Polydor 29/10/82
A. Pleasure Boys
B. The Anvil

1982. Der Amboss: 12" Promo Polydor
This was Steve's German language version of The Anvil. It was never officially released in the UK, but promotional copies were sent out to DJs.

1983. Fade To Grey Album: Polydor 10/83
The Singles Collection (A dance mix version of this album was also released)
1. Fade to Grey
2. Mind of a Toy
3. Visage
4. We Move
5. Tar
6. Der Amboss (Remix)
7. In the Year 2525
8. The Anvil
9. Night Train
10. Pleasure Boys
11. The Damned Don't Cry

1984. Single: Polydor 17/8/84
A. Love Glove
B. She's a Machine

1984. Beat Boy Album: Polydor 7/9/84
1. Beat Boy
2. Casualty
3. Questions
4. Only the Good (Die Young)
5. Can You Hear Me
6. The Promise
7. Love Glove
8. Yesterday's Shadow

1984. Single: Polydor 4/11/84
A. Beat Boy
B. Beat Boy (dance mix)

1985. Video: Polygram then Channel 5 Video
1. Visage
2. The Steps
3. Fade to Grey
4. Interview
5. The Dancer
6. The Damned Don't Cry
7. Pleasure Boys
8. Mind of a Toy
9. Whispers
10. Night Train
11. Can You Hear Me
12. Casualty
13. Intro
14. The Horseman
15. Yesterday's Shadow
16. Love Glove
17. Wild Life
18. Beat Boy
19. Can You Hear Me

1986. Single: EMI
A. Rebel Blue Rocker
B. Love Addiction

1986. Strange Cruise Album: EMI
1. Hit and Run
2. The Beat Goes On
3. Rebel Blue Rocker
4. Communication
5. This Old Town
6. Animal Call
7. Heart is a Lonely Hunter
8. Love Addiction
9. 12 Miles High
10. Where Were Their Hearts

1986. Single: EMI
A. The Beat Goes On
B. Silver Screen Queen

1988. Single: Virgin
With Roger Taylor as The Cross
Manipulator

1991. Single
This was Steve singing various Marc
Bolan songs, released by an
independent Marc Bolan fan.
Bolanesque

1993. Single: Polydor
Production team, The Bassheads,
released at least eight dance mixes of
Visage's greatest hit 16/8/93
Fade to Grey

1993. The Best of Visage Album
1. Fade to Grey
2. Mind of a Toy
3. Visage
4. We Move
5. Tar
6. In the Year 2525
7. The Anvil
8. Night Train
9. Pleasure Boys
10. The Damned Don't Cry
11. Love Glove
12. Fade to Grey (The Bassheads '93 7"
edit)

**1997: The Best of Visage Album –
Master Series: Polygram 1/9/97**
1. Fade To Grey

2. The Damned Don't Cry
3. Love Glove
4. Mind of a Toy
5. Der Amboss
6. Questions
7. Visage
8. The Promise
9. In the Year 2525
10. The Anvil
11. Beat Boy
12. The Steps
13. We Move
14. Only the Good Die Young
15. Motivation (a dance track added in
error – definitely not the Visage song!)
16. Blocks on Blocks

**2000. The Damned Don't Cry
Compilation Album: Spectrum
23/10/2000**
1. Visage
2. Tar
3. Fade to Grey
4. Mind of a Toy
5. Night Train
6. Whispers
7. The Anvil
8. We Move
9. Pleasure Boys
10. Love Glove
11. The Damned Don't Cry
12. Beat Boy
13. She's a Machine
14. In the Year 2525
15. Second Steps
16. Frequency 7

INDEX

Index